Kessing, Felix Maxwell

Social anthropology in
Polynesia: a review of
research

SOCIAL ANTHROPOLOGY IN POLYNESIA

SOCIAL ANTHROPOLOGY IN POLYNESIA

A Review of Research

FELIX M. KEESING

Professor of Anthropology
Stanford University

Published under the auspices of the
South Pacific Commission

GREENWOOD PRESS, PUBLISHERS
WESTPORT, CONNECTICUT

Library of Congress Cataloging in Publication Data

Keesing, Felix Maxwell, 1902-1961.
    Social anthropology in Polynesia.

    Reprint of the ed. published by Oxford University
Press, London, New York.
    Bibliography: p.
    Includes index.
    1. Ethnology--Polynesia. 2. Ethnology--Polynesia--
Bibliography. 3. Polynesia--Social conditions.
4. Polynesia--Social conditions--Bibliography.
I. Title.
[GN670.K43   1980]   996   80-17490
ISBN 0-313-22498-6 (lib. bdg.)

Reprinted in 1980 by Greenwood Press
A division of Congressional Information Service, Inc.
88 Post Road West, Westport, Connecticut 06881

Printed in the United States of America

10 9 8 7 6 5 4 3 2 1

The South Pacific Commission is an advisory and consultative body set up by the six Governments responsible for the administration of island territories in the South Pacific region. Its purpose is to recommend to the Member Governments means for promoting the well-being of the peoples of these territories. It is concerned with social, economic and health matters. Its headquarters are at Noumea, New Caledonia.

The Commission was established by an Agreement between the Governments of Australia, France, the Netherlands, New Zealand, the United Kingdom, and the United States of America, signed at Canberra on 6th February, 1947, and finally ratified on 29th July, 1948. Until 7th November, 1951, the area of the Commission's activities comprised territories lying generally south of the Equator from and including Netherlands New Guinea in the west to the French Establishments in Oceania and Pitcairn in the east. On 7th November, 1951, an additional Agreement was signed at Commission headquarters in Noumea on behalf of the six participating Governments, extending the scope of the Commission to include Guam and the Trust Territory of the Pacific Islands under the United States Administration.

The Commission consists of twelve Commissioners, two from each Government, and meets twice a year. The first Session was held in May 1948. There are two auxiliary bodies, the Research Council and the South Pacific Conference.

The Research Council, which assembles once a year, held its first meeting in May 1949. Members are appointed by the Commission, and are selected for their special knowledge of the questions with which the Commission is concerned, and the problems of the territories in these fields. The chief function of the Research Council is to advise the Commission what investigations are necessary. Arrangements to carry out those that are approved are the responsibility of the Secretary-General and other principal officers.

The South Pacific Conference, which meets at intervals not exceeding three years, consists of delegates from the local inhabitants of the territories, who may be accompanied by advisers. The first Conference was held in Suva in April 1950, and was attended by delegates from fifteen territories and from the Kingdom of Tonga.

CONTENTS

PREFACE

THIS STUDY forms one unit of a research project initiated by the South Pacific Commission as part of its Social Development research programme. The project was set up to provide a comprehensive survey of the work done to date in social anthropology as it relates to conditions and problems among the peoples of the South Pacific Territories, and to suggest lines for future research in this highly relevant scientific field.

The preparation of this unit of the survey forms part of the research programme in anthropology carried on within the Department of Sociology and Anthropology at Stanford University, California. A first draft of the text and bibliography was made in 1950, and distributed to a limited number of specialists for comments and suggestions. Subsequently I was able, as part of the work of a nine-month sabbatical leave trip to the South Pacific in 1950-51, to review the current situation and research needs at first hand in a number of the Territories concerned.

Besides consulting with anthropologists and others familiar with the region, I took the opportunity to check in detail the published works and unpublished manuscripts in libraries dealing with the area, notably at the Bernice P. Bishop Museum in Honolulu, Hawaii, the Mitchell Library in Sydney, Australia, and the Turnbull Library in Wellington, New Zealand, so as to round out the bibliography of relevant sources. This work was made possible as the result of a grant given by the Rockefeller Foundation, through Stanford University, to cover the expenses of the sabbatical leave trip. The present draft of the survey covers the situation and literature as known up to August 1951.

A first introductory chapter reviews the approach of "social anthropology" as a scientific discipline and offers a broad assessment of the nature and extent of work done to date within the South Pacific Territories being dealt with. Then follow three chapters analysing in greater detail the main types of problems of concern to the South Pacific Commission, in the economic, social, and health fields where its international responsibilities lie, on which social anthropology has in hand or can accumulate significant information.

The principles on which the bibliography has been built up are referred to in the preamble to the bibliographic section. Subject to certain factors of selection, particularly the elimination of the older and more marginal literature, it contains all references in the social anthropology field which could be located. It also gives a rough evaluation of their usefulness. All entries in the bibliography have been numbered for convenience of reference, and under each topical heading in the text references are made by these numbers to works in the bibliography which have most bearing on the problems concerned.

Chapter V contains a summary of further research needs, and offers suggestions as to priorities. It takes account of whether the work involved seems to be of a type most suitable for official sponsorship by the Commission or the constituent Governments, or else best left to private institutions and scholars. In some cases the proposed research is of a kind which specialists in social anthropology are used to doing wholly with their own professional "tools." But in others it would need to be done by anthropologists in collaboration with other specialists who have collateral expertness, e.g., in economics or in medicine, either through consultation, or by employing the new increasingly used "team" method of sending two or more specialists together into the field. The list of possible projects for future research is necessarily an exceedingly formidable one. It is hoped that, besides being useful as a guide to the Commission and to Governments, such an inventory can help to attract private institutions and individual scholars to work in the region by giving them some idea of the great range of relevant problems for future study.

Throughout the preparation of this survey, including the studies in the Territories, my wife, Marie Margaret Keesing, has acted as a collaborator. The typing of the manuscript was done most efficiently by Mrs. Patricia McEwen, Secretary of the Department of Sociology and Anthropology at Stanford University. Mr. Harry Maude, Executive Officer for Social Development, South Pacific Commission, gave useful advice and facilitated its issue in both its provisional and its final form.

Felix M. Keesing
Professor of Anthropology

Stanford University
California
August 10, 1951.

I

INTRODUCTORY

THE FOLLOWING report presents a summary of the work done to date in the field of Polynesian social anthropology, particularly as relevant to the programme and purposes of the South Pacific Commission, and also an estimate of further research needs and priorities.

The Region

The term "Polynesia" is here considered broadly. By the division of labour adopted for the project, Professor A. P. Elkin of the University of Sydney deals in his parallel survey with the main zone of "Melanesia," from New Guinea in the west to New Caledonia in the east.[1] This survey will cover not only the so-called Polynesian "triangle" of the central and eastern Pacific but also Fiji, which is a fringe area with both Polynesian and Melanesian affinities, and certain adjacent Micronesian areas which fall within the Commission's purview, (the Gilberts and Nauru).[2] A few scattered communities of dominantly Polynesian affiliation but situated on small islands within the Melanesian territories will also be referred to in this survey. Three important groups of Polynesians, however, are not directly included, as being outside the Territories within the scope of the South Pacific Commission: the New Zealand Maoris, the Hawaiians, and the people of Easter island (controlled by Chile). But comparative references to them are made both in the text and in the bibliography. For general works on the region being covered, see especially the bibliographic references numbered 5, 10, 27, 31, 36, 39, 40, 42, 53, 58, 65, 105, 106, 111, 113, 114, 123, 145, 160, 182.

The Approach of Social Anthropology

A preliminary word clarifying the approach of "social anthropology" will also be in order. This scientific label shuts out from reference certain types of anthropological study usually known as physical

---

[1] Elkin, A.P., *Social Anthropology in Melanesia: a Review of Research.*

[2] This survey was made before the Commission area was extended to include the United States Trust Territory of the Pacific Islands and Guam, which form the major part of Micronesia.

I

anthropology (racial origins and characteristics, *et cetera*), prehistoric archaeology,[3] and linguistics. For some anthropologists, "social anthropology" is fairly synonymous with "cultural anthropology," or the older term "ethnology," the study of "cultures" (that is, of local bodies of custom), though perhaps with emphasis on their non-material aspects. But others have preferred to think of "ethnology" as stressing the specific local history and geography of customs, and to count "social anthropology" as stressing more the basic under-standings which anthropologists can contribute to our accumulating social science knowledge about culture, society, and personality generally. Nevertheless, the finesse of scientific definition need not trouble us unduly here, and certainly not the often controversial theories and classifications of the various schools and scholars. The focus will be primarily upon those anthropological matters which have significance for the Commission's work programme.

The need for taking full account of the local settings of custom and thought among peoples such as those in the South Pacific has become axiomatic in relation to planning for welfare and development. It is often necessary, too, to go beyond common sense observation by getting aid from trained specialists, particularly in this case profession-ally trained anthropologists. Great progress has been made, even in the last decade, in methods of analysing custom and in discerning significant principles of "applied anthropology" which can be brought to bear upon administrative and other problems (see especially biblio-graphic references 12, 78, 105, 106, 110, 137, 143, 153). Governments increasingly find it useful, as in Africa, South and South-east Asia, Papua and New Guinea, the American-held islands of Micronesia, and some of the American countries, to maintain professional anthro-pologists on their staffs. Fortunately, too, anthropologists have become increasingly habituated to co-operation with government specialists and with scientists in other fields, particularly so as many of them have been actively engaged in military and civilian services during and since World War II.

In the Polynesian areas, a few anthropologists have been employed by administrations to date, but for short periods only. The smallness of the island territories and of the official staffs concerned has undoubted-ly been a deterrent to such appointments. The bulk of the work in

---

[3] Archaeological materials and their conservation are the subject of another South Pacific Commission project, "Archaeological and Historical Sites and Archives."

social anthropology, therefore, has been done by research workers primarily interested in academically oriented problems. When the test of practical needs is applied to their materials, gaps inevitably appear, and even much of what is available needs "processing" for it to become of fullest usefulness to the man of action. Furthermore, perhaps to a greater extent than in most comparable areas, students of Polynesia have focused attention upon matters rather remote from the present-day problems, such as the fascinating question of the origins and migrations of these island peoples, Stone Age technologies, folklore, and religious systems now largely obsolete. These types of study, of marked interest in reconstructing the past, are therefore heavily represented in the literature. Even so, the work done to date also contains a great amount of more relevant material which will be reviewed here, as on economic and social usages, demography, nutrition and other health matters, training of children, and "cultural dynamics" (change, and resistance to change) generally.

General Evaluation of Work to Date

Sir Peter H. Buck (Te Rangi Hiroa), formerly director of the well-known Bishop Museum in Honolulu, wrote in 1945 in his highly useful *Introduction to Polynesian Anthropology* that the general field survey of Polynesia had by then been "practically completed," and that publications were available covering virtually every phase of "history, legends, material culture, social organization, religion, and physical anthropology." Though the information, he says, may be "thin in parts," such weaknesses are "not due to the authors but to the fact that the native informants could not supply what they did not have" (36, p. 123).

Buck, who contributed so much himself to this impressive record, refers here to research primarily concerned with describing the pre-white cultures of the island peoples to the extent that this could be done in later times. But materials relating to post-white changes ("acculturation" in the jargon), and to the contemporary modes of life of these peoples, were interesting to most of the scholars concerned mainly as needing to be sifted out and discarded when necessary in the interests of reconstructing the genuinely old.

It is no criticism of this legitimate scientific effort to say that for the purpose of modern administrative application the discarded materials were likely to be those of greatest significance. Fortunately, over the last quarter century, a shift has occurred in the focus of academic anthropology which has fully legitimized studies both of cultural changes and of present-day modes and problems of living. The work of the Bishop Museum and of other scientific institutions interested in the Pacific has therefore increasingly taken account of the importance of recording materials of this kind, and a growing body of such information has become available. This is reviewed and summarized particularly in texts and bibliographies prepared by five scholars and published under the title *Specialized Studies in Polynesian Anthropology* (12, 43, 109, 112, 129), but such materials are still very far from complete, and from meeting the maximum potential of usefulness to administrations and to the Commission. This will be seen clearly in the following topical sections. Sir Peter Buck himself, in his work cited above, points out (pp. 126-28) some of these opportunities for further research in fields of cultural dynamics, the psychological dimensions of culture, and applied anthropology generally.

One factor which inevitably creates gaps in the existing information is the rapid development within social anthropology itself of new approaches for the study of such peoples and cultures. Most earlier ethnology, contributed to both by professional scholars and by officials, missionaries, and others for whom it was a serious avocation, consisted of building up a kind of inventory or mosaic of the separate elements of any given culture, and perhaps trying to trace the history of these "traits" in the past, and their geographic distribution in other cultures. Usually these materials have been published in scientific journals in a series of separate "papers" dealing with detailed items: agricultural techniques, fishhooks, marriage customs, rituals, and the many other matters of local custom. By this means, as will be seen from the bibliography, a cumulative picture gets filled out covering more or less fully any given culture in the region, along with its time and space background. Here and there a "monograph" in a scientific series or as a separate book brings together under one cover some larger segment, or gives a more superficial cataloguing of the culture as a whole. This work still goes on, and has validity within its limits if technically competent.

Since the 1920's, however, anthropologists have become increasingly dissatisfied with this type of descriptive or "historical" ethnology alone. It is weak in what science tends to count vital, a "sense of problem" (other than that of filling out the inventory), and misses out some of the dimensions of cultural study most important both for contemporary science and for practical application.

All sciences today, ranging from physics and chemistry to those dealing with human behaviour, now place great stress upon understanding the "structuring" or interrelationships of parts or units within a working and more or less "integrated" whole, whether it is the patterning of atoms and molecules, or, as in the case of social anthropology, the organized local system of culture and society that is Fijian, Samoan, and so on. Study is therefore focused not only on the many constituent elements of custom noted as making up this particular system of life, but also upon the "functional" or meaningful interrelations and characteristics that give them wholeness or "integration": the "patterning" of custom which defines what is normal and what deviant behaviour; the "configurations" as they are often called (value systems, needs, goals, themes, common denominator concepts, and other dimensions being investigated by different scholars) that provide consistencies of motivation to overt behaviour, and give wholeness and more or less uniqueness to the culture; the ways individuals become moulded from birth on to share in greater or less degree the range of personality (character structure) norms valued in the culture concerned; the detailed web of "social structure," or "interpersonal relations" that knits together the individuals into a "society"; and these, with their many more specific ramifications, within the dynamic setting of cultural change and administrative control characteristic of the island settings today.

Studies of the newer dimensions indicated in this inevitably rather jargonistic summary are little past their beginning in Polynesia today, and even in other areas they are still relatively few and highly experimental. Investigations of this kind call for an academic tough-mindedness on the part of anthropological workers, and a knowledge of various other scientific disciplines, particularly of psychology, that those trying out such approaches by no means always possess, so that such work is often open to criticism. Documenting such materials adequately is also a long and complex matter. But work of this kind will undoubtedly go forward in the area with increasing tempo as well as precision, and will be of benefit to those handling administrative and developmental problems. The main studies now available utilizing strongly these newer approaches in social anthropology are bibliographic references 136, 138, 217, 277, 295, 322, 323, 403, 455-457, 603-605, 883, 904-910.

Method of Analysis

The sections which follow will deal with what seem to be the most significant topics in the three fields of the Commission's interest: economic development, social development, and health. Some of these topics have been placed rather arbitrarily in a particular field, where in reality they concern two or even all three fields, e.g., "Population Numbers and Trends"; "Food Habits; Nutrition"; "Co-operative Activities." In several cases a significant subject for research has relevant materials scattered throughout the analysis, and so has not been separated out under any one topical heading, e.g., the problems associated with the important population elements of mixed ancestry, and also Asian immigrant groups; comprehensive studies of a given locality or community; "acculturation" (culture-contact) surveys.

Under each topical heading the anthropological information available to date is briefly evaluated, and references given by number to the main sources as listed in the bibliography. The needs and opportunities for further research in social anthropology are also examined.

Some projects are suggested for high priority in the development of the Commission's work programme, others are judged as having lower priority. The general principle used for guidance here is that, to be suitable for direct Commission sponsorship, a project should be of practical importance to welfare and development, and have wide regional significance that would make it of interest to at least a number, if not all, of the Territories concerned. In the case of some of the subjects discussed, there is less definiteness in terms of a practical problem focus, or else more local than regional application, so that they are better suited to research initiated by private institutions or individual scholars, or alternatively sponsored by the interested Government. Nevertheless, these subjects are frequently spelled out here as a necessary part of the background which the Commission-sponsored projects must take into account, e.g., study of social systems and ideologies. Furthermore, an analysis of these subjects in this context can help to meet that part of the Commission's assigned responsibilities concerned with co-operating with private institutions and scholars, and making them aware of basic research needs and possibilities.

Chapter V gives a summary tabulation of the research needs as outlined under the various topics, with emphasis upon means of execution and suggested priorities.

As regards personnel, many of the projects listed could be handled by persons competent in social anthropology working alone, as falling wholly within their familiar fields of reference. But for some, anthropologists could contribute most effectively by working in close collaboration with other technical specialists. In rare cases, it might be possible to secure anthropologists who are specialists in the topic concerned, and command at the same time the appropriate collateral knowledge relating to the subject so that they can take full responsibility. Conversely, for some problems, technicians in other fields might be available having enough collateral knowledge of social anthropology to deal with the subject concerned.

II

ECONOMIC DEVELOPMENT

ANTHROPOLOGISTS have emphasized, in their studies both of the indigenous cultures and of so-called acculturation, the "material culture" (technology) and economic organization characteristic of the island societies. Their investigations provide an essential background of custom and thought with which the technical approaches of experts in agriculture, fisheries, animal husbandry, forestry, marketing, and so on must be equated for successful operation.

Stress has been laid in the anthropological literature not only upon detailed facts about traditional production, distribution and consumption, but also upon basic differences in the less tangible "standards of living" characteristic of such non-Western economies and those of the West. Great contrasts appear in the definition of "wealth," "wants," "value," "price," "ownership," "work," "success," and other basic factors of economic organization and motivation. These have been most carefully examined by Firth, an anthropologist with training in economics (908, 936). Less fully treated, but still discussed by a number of writers, have been the modern changes taking place as such contrasting systems have met and interpenetrated, often with marked strains and stresses. These have been surveyed most comprehensively by Keesing (105, chapters VI-VII) and Oliver (145); see also 103, 166, 181, 931. The following sections deal with some of the main categories of economic welfare and development as seen from these anthropological viewpoints.

Adjustment to the Island Habitats

Anthropological writings usually contain considerable information relating to the island habitats and resources. These, partly based on locally gathered information, and partly selected from relevant scientific sources, typically cover subjects ranging from food getting and transport to settlement patterns and political boundaries.

Anthropologists, as others, have stressed the broad distinctions between "high" and "low" islands, the latter with a much more

8

limited range of resources with which to meet human needs. Several classic ethnological studies are available to show modes of living on small coral islands, e.g., the Beagleholes' monograph on Pukapuka (603); Buck on Tongareva (614) and Manihiki-Rakahanga (615); this subject will be discussed more fully on pp. 31ff. For high islands, important distinctions appear between those with coastal lagoons and reefs, e.g., Buck on Mangareva (811), Burrows on Uvea (596, 597), and those without such important sources of food and other products, e.g., Handy and Linton on the Marquesas (871, 882).

Variant island types within these broad categories are also shown to have interesting differences, including atolls, coral "pancakes," "raised" low islands, near-atolls with minor volcanic outcroppings, small and low volcanic islands, and so on to the very large island units such as Viti Levu in Fiji. Useful studies other than those mentioned are 205, 210, 245, 262, 295, 296, 298 (Fiji, including Lau and Rotuma); 323, 372 (Tonga); 386, 404, 441, 485 (Samoa); 520 (Tokelaus); 533, 534, 546, 550 (Gilberts and Ellices); 580, 581, 589 (Nauru); 595, 596, 597, 601 (Wallis and Horne); 603, 612, 614, 615, 616, 617 (Cooks); 655, 660 (Niue); 688, 691, 708, 756, 757 (Societies); 779, 780, 787 (Tuamotus); 811 (Gambiers or Mangareva); 828 (Australs); 848, 871, 882 (Marquesas); 907, 925 (Polynesian outliers in the Melanesian zone).

The anthropological viewpoint, taken together with the viewpoints of geography and related fields, suggests a usefulness for classifying these island habitats into several basic types. The following classification has emerged in the writer's studies as having considerable usefulness:

TYPE I

Small islets without adequate resources for permanent human habitation. Thousands of these exist in the area, and most are owned and visited by the peoples on larger adjacent islands so that their resources of land and sea are used; they therefore have some importance.

TYPE II

Small isolated islands or groups of islands, usually of low coral formation but sometimes volcanic, with limited resources and poor sea approaches. Sometimes densely inhabited proportionate to their size and potential of land and sea products, they offer a special challenge for welfare planning and research. In the modern setting there are likely to be few resident outsiders other than officials, missionaries and perhaps traders at a few points, and even visitors come rarely. Into this type would fall most or all of the Gilbert and Ellice groups (other than Ocean Island), the Phoenixes, Tokelaus, the Laus, most of the Cooks, Niue, the Tuamotus (except Makatea), the Australs, and many islands in the other groups.

TYPE III

Small islands or island zones, with special commercial resources or military or other facilities which bring about greatly accelerated development. Instances are Nauru, Ocean, and Makatea which have large scale phosphate workings, the Pago Pago harbour area in American Samoa, the Nandi airport area in Fiji, and Canton Island in the Phoenixes. Any indigenous populations in such zones have been subject to greatly accelerated culture-contact, not least of all because of proximity to Europeans and perhaps Asiatic labourers involved in these special enterprises. The cases of Ocean and Nauru (532, 533, 566, 581) illustrate particularly how financial and other resources may be much more readily available for local welfare and development activities than in other areas.

TYPE IV

Larger islands or island zones, usually of mainly volcanic structure, with more diversified resources, but still isolated and relatively little developed. The indigenous settlements in such areas are often sparse and scattered irregularly in the few most favourable and accessible spots. This type generally lacks good harbours or other sea approaches, and is likely to have little road development. Correlated with this poverty in communications, European and other settlers from outside are likely to be at a minimum and confined to a few places. Notable examples are Samoa's biggest island, Savai'i; the large islands of the Marquesas, and considerable sections of the main islands of Fiji, especially those other than Viti Levu. In the long distant future some of the empty sections in these areas, properly opened up, may be colonized from the more crowded zones of the islands, provided, of course, arrangements can be made with present owners to admit such outsiders.

TYPE V

The few larger islands or island zones in which extensive or considerable economic development has already taken place along modern lines. These are served by at least reasonably good harbour facilities. Besides some degree of urban development at the port or ports, they have accessible hinterlands in which commercial and industrial activities can thrive. The latter may comprise larger-scale plantations, mining enterprises, and perhaps commercial utilization of sea and forest products, these likely to be run mainly by European owners using island or Asiatic labour. In territories where Asiatics are allowed to become independent holders, they may buy or lease land in such areas and spread out mainly as small farmers and tradesmen. Here public works and other modern facilities find their main focus, so that even indigenous communities near the centres may have electric lights, water systems, and other amenities denied to outer settlements. It is in such settings that population tends to be increasing most rapidly, both by natural growth and immigration. So-called acculturation or culture-change is also at its maximum in economic, social, educational and other respects, with its progress likely to be roughly proportionate to the distance and accessibility of each community to the urban centre. Included here obviously are much of New Caledonia and of Viti Levu island in Fiji, both with a number of urban centres, also the north coast of Upolu island around Apia in Western Samoa, much of Tahiti island, especially around Papeete, and to a lesser degree the Nukualofa region in Tonga and the Avarua region in Rarotonga. It may be noted that the actual urban centres could form a separate category, Type VI, under any such scheme.

A classification of this sort not only helps to focus attention on differential conditions and problems existing in the islands, but also may be of aid in choosing the locale for pilot studies in various fields of needed research. In general, anthropological studies in the area to date have concentrated most upon groups living under Type II and Type IV conditions. But many of the most serious problems occur under Type III and Type V conditions. For a comparable analysis of habitats in the adjacent islands of American Micronesia see 941, chapters II, III, with accompanying references.

Population Numbers and Trends

Anthropologists have accumulated considerable materials relating to the basic demographic features which must form the background for all studies in fields of health, economic development, and social development, and this type of data is particularly stressed in contemporary anthropological studies. It must be said immediately, however, that the available information, anthropological and otherwise, still falls far short of what should be known. The following are main sources: 44, 87, 105, 116, 163, 182 (general); 205, 221, 227, 230, 248, 252, 253, 263, 277, 281, 295, 308 (Fiji); 323, 344, 367, 372 (Tonga); 427, 438, 454, 511 (Samoa); 519, 520 (Tokelaus); 534, 536, 552 (Gilberts and Ellices); 581, 591 (Nauru); 595, 596, 601 (Wallis and Horne); 603, 614, 615, 616, 620, 636, 639 (Cooks); 660 (Niue); 679, 681, 708, 742, 758 (Societies); 789, 800 (Tuamotus); 811 (Gambiers); 828 (Australs); 852, 853, 866, 871, 892, 901 (Marquesas); 907, 911, 922 (Polynesian outliers).

The anthropologist is aware of the difficulties faced by the census taker, amateur or professional, in such areas: problems of accurate counting and age reckoning, the migratory habits of many groups, and possible suspicions and distortions. His own counts are ideally calculated from intimate genealogical and other family studies; but except on small islands (e.g., Firth for Tikopia, 907) they yield only intensive samples (e.g., the Beagleholes' Pangai village, 323). Given, however, such census materials as are available on historical trends in total population, also any modern figures for age and sex distributions, and records of births, deaths, and migration, he may do a fair job of analysis as to their scientific and practical applications, e.g., a summary by Keesing (105, pp. 43-65, 306-09). Such analysis of population trends has been particularly stressed in numerous recent anthropological studies made in the United States Trust Territory under the so-called CIMA (Co-ordinated Investigation of Micronesian Anthropology) and SIM (Scientific Investigations in Micronesia) projects sponsored by the Pacific Science Board of the U.S. National Research Council (see 941, chapter IV).

Anthropological works are likely to yield most or all of what can now be known, whether extensive or meagre, of the early historical background of population: numbers, ecological patterns, fertility and mortality, sex and other customs affecting birth and survival, race mixture in early days of Western contact, depopulation through new diseases and other destructive factors, and other relevant matters. For the more modern period, however, the approaches of the anthropologist can most profitably be made a matter of team work with medical and economic specialists.

Analyses by Hogbin, Keesing, and others have shown birth rates under indigenous conditions to be typically high by modern Western standards, and often very high; yet for some groups they are sometimes medium, or even occasionally low. Unfortunately, too little is known in detail about these fertility differences, but local custom clearly enters in as shown by limited studies to date. Among recognized factors are the extent of adolescent sex experimentation, age of marriage, habits of coitus, artificial controls, the securities afforded in family settings, and disease conditions. This is a field which might lend itself particularly to work by private institutions, preferably with a medical-anthropological team, especially to examine the possibilities of lowering high birth rates to match falling death rates.

While birth rates have tended to remain at a persistent level, with social customs and other factors from the traditional setting continuing to operate strongly, death rates have been subject to marked fluctuations. Under indigenous conditions they evidently tended, through high infant mortality, accident, war, and other lethal factors to parallel the birth rates, making for a population balance, or if surpluses developed, migration usually had to take place. The early population records of a number of the small Pacific islands show an extraordinary degree of stability in numbers over several generations. (Incidentally, anthropologists reject strongly a pseudo-scientific theory formerly having some currency that the Polynesians were already declining through degeneration when Europeans arrived.) With Western contacts, death rates usually soared because of epidemics, acceleration of wars, perhaps psycho-somatic strains and stresses, and other factors often discussed in the literature. This brought a population decline which appears to have reached its most serious proportions in the Marquesas, at least until recently (citations above).

But modern health measures and new securities have tended in turn to force down mortality strongly, so that by now, in nearly all areas of the central and eastern Pacific, births exceed deaths and population is gaining. Typically, the island populations now have a much larger proportion in the pre-reproductive and early reproductive age groups than in mature Western populations, hence a prospect of continuing increase perhaps at an accelerating rate in the immediate generations. The extreme case is American Samoa where current trends suggest that the indigenous population, which has more than doubled in the past two decades, will double again well within the next two decades; the Samoans of Western Samoa are also increasing almost as rapidly.

The economic and social (including educational) implications of such population trends are clear enough to warrant giving them high priority for further research. There are still places where population tends to be stationary, and possibly decreasing, though the latter problem is now almost wholly confined to the areas of more recent contact in Melanesia. But the potentially serious problems are those associated with overpopulation.

Already, for example, Gilbertese atoll dwellers have needed to spill over into the Phoenix islands, and other small islands such as the Tokelaus appear to be feeling the pinch. Even in the larger Samoa group certain areas, especially those in and around the towns of Apia and Pago Pago, are densely populated in terms of current economic patterns, with gardens spread far up on the mountain heights; patients have been admitted to the hospital of American Samoa through literally falling out of cliffside plantations. Where for so long population vigour as expressed in numerical increase has tended to be a yardstick for success in health work and other aspects of administration, it is becoming increasingly clear that, for such ocean-bound islands, measures designed to discourage high fertility and meet the problems of potential overpopulation are becoming more important yardsticks. Further anthropological research focused on these problems, preferably in close collaboration as indicated already with medical, economic and educational specialists, should be able to yield important practical leads to guide future policy. The whole field of demographic research is, of course, relevant to the Commission's programme.

Agriculture

Economists may well be surprised to find how much material exists in the anthropological literature bearing on agricultural production.

The importance of gardens and orchards in the indigenous economy led to extensive recording of the plants involved; their local names; production methods; their handling and consumption, and their social and religious associations. The following are main sources: 63, 108, 166 (general); 204, 205, 221, 262, 269, 271, 273, 277, 295, 296, 298, 319 (Fiji); 323, 361, 372 (Tonga); 388, 394, 404, 417, 427, 429, 438, 441, 469, 485 (Samoa); 519, 520 (Tokelaus); 528, 534, 546, 547, 550, 568 (Gilberts and Ellices); 581, 584, 588, 591 (Nauru); 595, 596, 597, 601 (Wallis and Horne); 603, 612, 614, 615, 617, 620, 622 (Cooks); 655, 660, 661 (Niue); 681, 683, 691, 708, 741, 755, 763 (Societies); 784, 789 (Tuamotus); 811 (Gambiers); 828 (Australs); 871, 882, 892 (Marquesas); 908, 910, 925 (Polynesian outliers).

The importance of the coconut palm and its products, especially for the low islands, is fully stressed. Buck's study of Manihiki and Rakahanga (615), for example, shows the complex nomenclature of the coconut for an atoll people who depend so much upon it, and also the amazingly varied foods and other products which it can yield. Handy's classic study of the taro (937) shows particularly the many species of this plant, with their varied growing conditions, and also the different methods of production and use. The cultivation of coarse types of taro or more often of the taro-like "puraka" (*Cyrtosperma chamissonis*), in pits on low islands is well documented, especially by Buck in his Cook island studies. Other plant foods, among them indigenous types such as yams, sweet-potatoes, bananas, breadfruit, and pandanus (a staple food on some of the low islands), and ones introduced later such as manioc, corn, papaia, and pineapples, each have varied references. So, too, have other useful plants such as sugar cane for thatching, the paper-mulberry for bark cloth, tobacco, and the kava from the root of which many groups make a ceremonial drink. Possibly a master index might be prepared at some time in the future to make this information more accessible.

Descriptions of cultivation methods show general likenesses but also significant variants. Because the focus of most studies is on the traditional systems, it is not always clear whether the older methods are fully in use today or have been modified (e.g., the tools employed; the survival of older magical ideas and practices). Furthermore, reference may be inadequate regarding new plant introductions and the adaptations they have brought about (e.g., coffee and cocoa in some places), and also resistance to new products (e.g., the general failure to adopt rice culture). But several useful analyses of contemporary agriculture are available, notably for Fiji by Geddes (221), Quain (277), and Thompson (295, 298), and for Tonga by the Beagleholes (323). Furthermore, a few anthropological writers have discussed the modern situation more broadly in terms of subsistence needs, commercial developments, government activities, and potentials for the future in view of population increase, marketing prospects, and other factors: see especially 105, 108, 145, 295, 323, 438, 606, 608. Materials of this type are particularly extensive for the neighbouring island areas of American Micronesia where a number of studies have been made in the post-war period by the United States Commercial Company and Pacific Science Board scientists (see especially 941).

Matters relative to land tenure, organization of work, and food habits are discussed later in this economic development section, and co-operative activities under social development. In terms of the potential contributions of workers in social anthropology, the following are some of the topics under the heading of agriculture which might profitably be projects for research in sample areas: expert local knowledge relating to important plant crops, keeping in mind the possibility of disseminating regionally any new and stimulating ideas and practices; present garden and orchard development in relation to population numbers and trends; problems involved in extension of gardens and orchards into new areas; problems associated with motivating disease and pest control by islanders; problems involved in introducing technical improvements in handling and marketing local produce; the present social and religious contexts of agricultural activities; a general assessment of the impact of "extension" programmes undertaken by governments to date, including the work and role of indigenous agricultural employees. For some types of research it has been found advantageous in American Micronesia to have anthropologists work with soil scientists, agronomists, economists, and other specialists, the former probing the context of local custom and thought relating to the technical matters with which the others are most competent to deal: for example, the ecology of plants and cultivations, fertilization methods, mechanization, and grading standards.

Anthropologists in the South Pacific have concentrated to date upon the indigenous peoples. But their colleagues in India, China, and South-east Asia have made studies of the systems of agriculture among the peoples of those areas. Correspondingly, it would be feasible for parallel studies to be made of such immigrant groups as the Indian farmers of Fiji, or Chinese, Indo-Chinese, and Javanese farmers in the French territories. So far the activities and problems of these often important population elements have not been recorded to any extent with the intimacy of anthropological studies, though there is some literature, e.g., Coulter's brief surveys of Fiji's Indians (204, 205). A further study of Indians in Fiji is currently in progress by an anthropologist of the Australian National University. A later discussion of "The Independent Smallholder" (see pp. 33-5) is particularly relevant to these problems.

Marine Products

As would be expected from the important place of fishing in the life of these islanders, especially of reef and shore fisheries, the anthropological literature has a great amount of material on the utilization of marine products: fish, shell, and edible marine plants. The monographs of the Bishop Museum are especially detailed in describing hooks and gorges, nets, traps, weirs, corrals, poisons, and other fish catching devices, often with carefully drawn diagrams. These and other sources are also likely to contain the local names of marine animals and plants; methods of preparing and using marine products, and the larger economic and social setting of such activities. The following are main sources: 1, 14, 15, 71, 84, 85, 145 (general); 207, 221, 277, 296, 305, 306 (Fiji); 323 (Tonga); 388, 395, 407, 422, 427, 441, 473, 492, 494, 500, 508 (Samoa); 519 (Tokelaus); 529, 534, 542, 550 (Gilberts and Ellices); 581, 585, 590, 591 (Nauru); 595, 596, 597, 601 (Wallis and Horne); 603, 612, 613, 614, 615, 617, 619, 643 (Cooks); 660 (Niue); 678, 680, 709, 735, 738, 748, 751, 762 (Societies); 771, 784, 799 (Tuamotus); 811 (Gambiers); 828 (Australs); 830, 862, 870, 871, 882 (Marquesas); 903, 908, 923, 925 (Polynesian outliers).

Any Commission project dealing with fisheries, whether for subsistence or commercial purposes, would do well to take full account of this material, not least of all because the local fish are actually caught by such indigenous methods, which cannot always be said when methods developed for fishing elsewhere are transferred to the island settings. Many of these empirically discovered techniques of the islanders have wide regional distribution, though usually with minor local variations. There are also special local techniques which could possibly be made known in other island areas with profit. Just as islanders have so often readily borrowed useful new ideas when presented to them, they might become interested in adopting and adapting new fishing techniques to their profit if means could be found of disseminating such information through specimens, slides, simple diagrams, and appropriate text materials.

A considerable decline in fishing characterizes most of the island areas in modern days. This is referred to frequently but summarily in the literature, e.g., only one fish trap was found remaining on Mangaia, Cook Islands, when Dr. Buck made a study in 1926. A number of writers have mourned the substitution of canned goods instead, considering the scarcity of fresh fish as a backward step in nutrition. But no careful study is available of the circumstances through which fishing has been diminished or abandoned, or of the extent to which it might be stimulated or revived.

Some open sea fishing was done by islanders. This may still be carried on, as in most parts of Samoa, though apparently everywhere throughout the islands it has tended to decline. The traditional methods of open sea fishing were necessarily limited to small boats operating near the shore, so that the techniques involved would presumably have at most only limited application for any larger-scale operations of modern commercial character. Yet even here the islanders' knowledge of baits, the habits of fish, and local waters, could profitably be drawn upon wherever such enterprises are contemplated. Not much of this kind of information, however, is yet recorded. The problem might well exist here of getting the co-operation of the local peoples: they might need to be assured that their own fish supplies would not become depleted, as with the bait fish that are part of the balance of shore and reef fish life, and that the profits from local fishing would not accrue wholly to outsiders.

Emphasis has recently been laid by fisheries experts on the value of pond fisheries. The Gilbertese have fish ponds, but otherwise none of the islanders in this area appear to "cultivate" fish in ponds in anything like the systematic ways that were used by some of the peoples in South-east Asia and also by the Hawaiians. Some islanders had small artificial ponds for rearing and keeping turtles for food, but for the rest they used any available lagoons, stream pools and occasional inland lakes as natural "ponds" for salt and fresh water fish. Even the

Hawaiians soon ceased to work their stone-walled fish ponds in post-white times, leasing them out to Chinese and others to be used or letting them fall into disrepair. Modern methods of pond culture may become significant for some of the Europeans, part-islanders, and Asiatic settlers. But it is exceedingly dubious that the island peoples would quickly adopt, beyond a possible passing fad, any pool fishery techniques which require frequent heavy work or complicated new skills. In their case, attention may best be concentrated in this matter upon methods of improving and developing the traditional lagoon and stream fisheries.

The Western technical expert will sometimes need to be the learner instead of the teacher as regards marine products, and here the anthropologist can be of partial help. This may be true of any local use of edible sea plants (nearly always lumped by the European into the general category of "seaweeds"). It may also apply to the use and knowledge of the living habits of shellfish from which commercially valuable shell is obtained, and any other local marine products such as trepang (*bêche-de-mer*, or sea-slug) or fancy corals for which markets may be found.

Livestock

Though perhaps most thought of in connexion with immigrant groups, this aspect of the island economies has a minor but not unimportant place in the indigenous setting of life. The older anthropological works were usually content to list the domesticated animals present in pre-white times—usually the dog, pig, and chicken—and their place in the larder. Several of the recent works, however, devote some space to the number and care of livestock in the village settings, e.g. Beaglehole (323), Coulter (205), Geddes (221), Keesing (438), Quain (277), Thompson (295, 298).

Some of the low islands have a minimum of domestic animals, old or new, as the food resources are usually lacking to maintain them in numbers. On higher islands, however, as in Fiji, Tonga, Samoa, and Tahiti, horses of nondescript breeds may be used now for riding, but especially for transport to distant plantations (in the case of Tonga, harnessed to small carts). Scrub cattle and goats may also at least help in keeping plantations clear. Control of pigs has always been a problem, the more so as they now run wild on some islands and are destructive to gardens; but the pig also enters deeply into the local custom in many places as having ceremonial significance and being used for feast food. Domestic dogs and fowls, nondescript in breed, are likely to get little care. Rarely, as in Fiji, an enterprising islander may match immigrant farmers in having horses or cattle for farm work, and cattle or goats for flesh and dairy products. Some families, especially around the ports, have become used to drinking milk, or are at least giving milk to the children, but this is likely to come from cans.

Most indigenous communities, it may be noted, occupy wet belts where taro and other agricultural crops will thrive with minimum or no artificial irrigation. Such conditions are generally unfavourable for grasses suited to pasturage. Attempts to improve tropical grazing for livestock are likely, therefore, to be of greater significance at the present time to individual settlers, especially in drier zones, rather than to indigenous villagers, though of course not wholly so. The improvement of livestock breeds is primarily a technical problem, but programmes designed for such purposes may also involve factors of motivation and of cultural context generally in which anthropological studies could be of help.

Hand-crafts

The traditional arts and crafts are usually given detailed treatment in anthropological works, generally under the rubric "material culture" in monographs, and otherwise mostly in small, widely scattered papers. The Bulletins of the Bishop Museum give particularly good examples of careful reporting on tools, utensils, plaiting, and other craft work. Much less information is available on their modern status, both for local uses and for the often important commercial production in those territories where market outlets have opened up. The following are main sources: 23, 33, 39, 52, 58, 69, 83, 102, 118, 123, 135, 144, 146, 158, 179 (general); 206, 221, 243, 245, 247, 260, 262, 264, 268, 279, 292, 296, 301 (Fiji); 323, 329, 330, 344, 348, 370 (Tonga); 388, 390, 426, 427, 441, 451, 473 (Samoa); 519, 520 (Tokelaus); 534, 546, 550, 562, 565, 573 (Gilberts and Ellices); 581, 582, 586, 590 (Nauru); 595, 596, 601 (Wallis and Horne); 603, 612, 614, 615, 617, 621, 633, 645, 648, 649 (Cooks); 660, 661 (Niue); 675, 677, 698, 708, 711 (Societies); 767, 779, 780, 784, 789, 800 (Tuamotus); 811, 827 (Gambiers); 828, 830, 833, 835, 836, 840 (Australs); 846, 850, 855, 862, 867, 871, 882, 892, 895 (especially volume II), 899, 900 (Marquesas); 909, 925 (Polynesian outliers).

Inevitably, some of the old-time hand-crafts became obsolete with culture-contact, as with making stone tools, and in some areas even building canoes, and the general trend is in this direction with the availability of trade goods. But to a surprising extent they still survive, either in their full traditional setting such as plaiting mats for daily use, or in modified form as with making tapa (bark cloth) for some continuing practical uses such as screens and bedding, and for ceremonial or commercial purposes, but no longer for everyday clothing. New crafts have also come in, sometimes under commercial stimulus, as with making tortoise-shell ornaments or working silver. The average villager is likely now to be competent with the modern saw, chisel, and sewing machine, and many individuals have become expert in building and other trade pursuits. All such adjustments in hand-craft work have repercussions, as many scholars have pointed out, upon the larger economic and social settings of life.

Sample studies would be pertinent to show the present situation and context of arts and crafts in selected island communities. One approach in this matter could be directly commercial, investigating the marketing and other possibilities of developing local hand-crafts for sale. This appears to have a high priority in view of the basic need for diversifying production and stabilizing and expanding money income. Some hand-crafts are particularly adapted to women's work, and so offer women an independent source of income. Some governments have instituted training schemes to improve hand-craft standards and a record of the degree of success achieved by these efforts would be most useful. Too often the making of cheap curios with poor workmanship and disharmonious colours replaces the finer craft standards of which the people are capable. It is not often realized that objects of genuine artistic quality could command much higher prices if brought within the market for art work. Along with the commercial aspect, consideration should also be given to the social importance of arts and crafts, referred to frequently in the anthropological literature as providing constructive means of leisure and self-expression, and of giving a sense of worth and integrity to the individual (see "Art and Leisure" p. 48).

An aspect of hand-craft development which may be important, or even essential to craft continuity, is the availability of first-class raw materials. Some islands are known already to have shortages. Technical studies are needed, where not already made, of the best local types of pandanus, paper-mulberry, and other sources of craft materials, their availability, and their possible improvement, as perhaps through inter-island distribution of better types.

Forestry

Anthropological works include sporadic information relating to the nature and particularly the utilization by indigenous communities of forest resources. This may include local names for trees and other plants; description of the specific uses of wood or fibres in terms of their different qualities; reference to any nuts, seeds, gums, or other products, edible or otherwise useful; materials on birds and other wild game; and analysis of property rights and customs involved. Significant references in anthropological and related studies are found in 6, 49, 71, 151, 159, 269, 271, 273, 296, 319, 388, 441, 485, 578, 590, 612, 617, 711, 741, 755, 811, 818, 882, 908, 925.

Anthropologists can contribute only minor collateral materials to the professional forester, e.g., the uses made of forest materials and products by local communities; information on the desirable qualities and availability of plants used for hand-crafts; the customary setting of property rights in a given forest area.

Food Habits; Nutrition

This vital topic overlaps all three fields of the Commission's interest: the health field as bearing particularly on dietary adequacy for adults and children; economic development as being concerned with production and distribution, also the improvement of foodstuffs; social development as concerned with the social contexts of food habits, e.g., tastes, daily eating habits, ceremonial aspects of consumption. For most of these problems some anthropological information exists and anthropologists are capable of making fuller contributions in co-operation with the other specialists involved.

A useful general manual on this topic is available, prepared by a Food Habits Committee of the U.S. National Research Council, under the chairmanship of Dr. Margaret Mead, well known anthropologist (Washington, 1943). As regards the anthropological literature directly dealing with the island territories, the following are main sources: 6, 17, 63, 71, 81, 142, 151, 155, 159, 169, 180, 188 (general); 205, 221, 251, 262, 268, 269, 271, 273, 277, 283, 289, 295, 319 (Fiji);

323, 336, 345, 356 (Tonga); 388, 401, 404, 427, 430, 441, 455, 473, 476, 485, 488, 492, 503 (Samoa); 519, 520 (Tokelaus); 534, 540, 546, 547, 550, 552, 564 (Gilberts and Ellices); 581, 582, 591 (Nauru); 595, 596, 601 (Wallis and Horne); 603, 606, 612, 614, 615, 617, 620, 636 (Cooks); 660, 661 (Niue); 691, 709, 721, 741, 762, 763 (Societies); 789, 800 (Tuamotus); 811, 815, 818 (Gambiers); 828 (Australs); 871, 882, 883, 892 (Marquesas); 907, 908, 922, 925 (Polynesian outliers).

This material usually contains fairly full descriptions of foods, their preservation, and their preparation. Reference is also made to often significant distinctions between everyday foods and ceremonial foods used for feasting or for religious purposes; emergency foods used in times of famine or other deprivation; alcoholic and narcotic drinks, especially palm toddies and infusions of kava root (*piper methysticum*, 188), and medicinal foods. Anthropologists have ventured to suggest that the dietary balance of many groups in this zone of the islands appears to have been a very good one under indigenous conditions, a view which has some support from current nutritional research. They have also offered scattered comments on dietary changes brought about in modern days, especially the coming of trade goods, with often deleterious results as disturbing the dietary patterns; introduction of new plant and animal foods, and the diet of labouring groups.

Less fully treated, but given in a few of the more recent studies, are more or less detailed analyses of actual food intake per individual in the manner of a technical level of living study or nutritional survey. The most precise anthropological surveys available of actual diet appear to be in the Beagleholes' Pangai village study in Tonga (323), Firth's economic survey of Tikopia (907, 908), Quain's Fijian village study (277), and Thompson's Lau work (295, 298).

To a nutritionist, however, even studies of this type may be too vague as a basis for measuring dietary adequacy unless supplemented by further detailed quantitative and qualitative analysis. Yet the nutritionist who tries to make a conventional type of survey in such societies is likely to come up against unexpected and almost insuperable difficulties of record: often markedly different meal schedules from those of Westerners, with perhaps more, perhaps less meals per day, or again very erratic intake of food; the contrasts mentioned above between everyday food and ceremonial food; status differentiations, as between high and low born people, perhaps males and females,

C

old and young; odd snacks taken at all hours wherever nuts, raw fish or other foods may become available; differing liquid intake, and other variables.

Infant nutrition is usually recorded in summary fashion only, along perhaps with references to the "correct" diet for the mother before and after the birth and any attendant magical or other practices supposedly helpful (e.g., 295, 323, 503, 564, 883). The mother's milk, or that of a wet nurse, may be supplemented early with the jelly-like flesh of the unripe coconut, partially masticated banana or taro chewed by the mother, or other local foods. A baby may be encouraged to chew on rather hard lumps of taro. Weaning is likely to occur later than by Western practice, but is still a health crisis; occasional suckling may continue for years. In many groups children, once weaned, do not appear to get regularly or carefully fed and may have to subsist on left-overs from elders. But all these matters require more sharply focused observation than anthropologists have given them in the more general surveys to date. The techniques of anthropological study are invaluable in all such dietary investigations, and it seems essential to have these skills represented on any Commission team, whether dealing with adult or infant nutrition, along with economic, medical, and nutritional expertness.

One quite concrete problem in which anthropologists could give direct help is the important matter of preserving and storing foods. The perishable nature of most of the familiar foodstuffs, combined with climatic conditions, insect ravages, and other factors, militate against keeping them for more than a few hours, and even then the risks of contamination or deterioration are great. It undoubtedly contributes to the often discussed stereotype of the islander as "wasteful" or prodigal in his food habits. Nevertheless, some techniques are in local use for drying, salting, pickling, fermenting, or otherwise preserving certain foods (e.g., 169). One example is the use by some groups of underground pits for fermenting and preserving breadfruit, bananas, or certain other plant foods. Processes of this kind might be recorded more fully with the object of disseminating knowledge of them more widely, provided they meet reasonable health standards. Further improvements in food preservation and storage could well be made a high priority subject for research.

Another dietary problem which has aroused some discussion is whether the conventional island diets are deficient for maintaining workers on regular wage-earning jobs. It has been suggested that many labourers suffer from "hidden" hungers that impair efficiency, especially for undertaking prolonged hard work. Some workers may eat little if anything during the day because their customary main meal comes at night. Where food is supplied to a labour force by employers, it has often been nutritionally inadequate, though less so nowadays because of government regulations. This matter of the relation between work and diet appears to be of growing importance in all island areas, and might be given high priority for Commission study; it is one in which an anthropologist could profitably be a co-worker with medical personnel.

Trade and Commerce

This topic is partly covered under the heading of "Co-operative Activities" in the social development section. The economic and social background to co-operative societies and other types of modern trading is fairly extensively reviewed in anthropological literature, particularly its indigenous dimensions. But it is usually scattered in brief items under various topical heads. Among the most significant references are 78, 95, 106, 108, 166, 205, 221, 258, 268, 272, 277, 293, 295, 323, 361, 388, 438, 441, 458, 557, 568, 580, 603, 608, 688, 699, 871, 908.

It is well known that, until Europeans arrived, these islands of the Pacific were outside the Eurasian zone of distribution of well developed commercial concepts and practices, even though these were generally present in western Pacific areas. Traditional exchanges of most goods and services were highly personalized within household, kin, and community groups. Reciprocal give-and-take was the rule, often through what anthropologists call "gift exchanges," and usually with little overt development of impersonal transactions, markets, "profit," "interest," or the use of common denominators of exchange (money). So-called "moneys" of shell, teeth, mats, stone, or other materials had social and ceremonial functions rather than the full connotations of modern money. The best discussion of likenesses and contrasts between Polynesian and European practices is by Firth (908); they are also variously discussed by the Beagleholes (323), Keesing (105, 438), Oliver (145), Thompson (295), and others.

The coming of Europeans, creating new wants and introducing new goods, has been described by anthropologists and others as bringing about everywhere quick adaptations in traditional custom to make room for the trader. The islanders correspondingly learned to produce a limited range of goods, particularly copra, up to the measure of their slowly increasing needs. But older usages of distribution and exchange have also tended to persist strongly in local economic affairs. Only recently are marked signs of deterioration showing, mostly around the urban settings and even then mainly among the educated minority.

Commercial production by islanders today is closely geared to immediate and still limited needs. This shows vividly in high volume output when prices fall, and low volume output when they rise. Only slowly are the concepts of measuring success by savings and surpluses, or judging the worth of individuals by their personal achievements and income, making headway. In all these matters, recent official policies have usually tried to achieve a balance between protection of the islanders for welfare reasons and development for general territorial advancement. All such problems are sporadically treated in anthropological literature; the most comprehensive summaries are by Keesing (105, chapter VII) and Oliver (145).

The anthropologist would not claim expertness in trade techniques such as the problems of grading and marketing. He can, however, contribute much more than has been done to date on the economic and social contexts of present-day commercial development. An anthropologist might here work with profit as part of any team which would include the technical specialists most closely involved. This aspect of anthropological study appears to deserve high priority as background for the Commission's work programme in commercial fields, and could be the subject of one or more pilot studies. It may be noted that it has been emphasized in post-war studies by anthropologists in the collateral area of American Micronesia (941).

Money and Credit

So-called island "moneys" were referred to in the previous section. The place of modern money in the island economies is the subject of scattered comments in the literature, and of general discussions by Keesing (105) and Oliver (145). The use of money is shown as selectively, though deeply, interpenetrating the traditional modes of exchanging goods and services (e.g. marriage gifts, ceremonial displays of wealth); it is also obviously needed for participation in the larger life of the territory (e.g., for purchase of trade goods, payment of taxes, mission contributions). But the subject is so important as to deserve much fuller study.

Anthropologists can also explore certain aspects of the present use and potential needs for capital and credit. Much has been made popularly of the "happy-go-lucky" and "thriftless" islander whose savings bank is his garden, the ocean, and his relatives. Most territories have regulated strictly the advancing of credit, not only to protect the local people from being exploited but also as a protection against financial irresponsibility and inexperience. Yet a minority of individuals, sometimes islanders but often part-islanders, are tending to acquire the financial ambitions and motivations of the West, and their spheres of influence are expanding actively. This has, from the viewpoint of welfare, both good and bad possibilities, on the one hand making for development, but on the other involving dangers of exploitation of the less experienced by such persons. Banks are being increasingly used for savings and credit, or needed where they do not exist. This topic, particularly as relating to capital and credit, might well be made a high priority subject for one or more pilot studies under Commission auspices, to be undertaken in part by anthropologists, working with economists. It could be conjoined with studies relating to trade and commerce (see previous section).

Transportation

Local sea transport today is carried on to a considerable extent by indigenous style craft, or modifications of such craft, utilizing maritime skills of largely traditional derivation. This sometimes applies to inter-island traffic, as well as to intra-lagoon traffic, fishing, and other local activities. For landing on coasts with difficult reef and shore approaches, as on some of the low islands, local seamanship knowledge is still highly important.

In general, however, use of the older types of outrigger canoes and other local craft has diminished because of the availability of Western style craft. The usually detailed reports of anthropologists on boats, boat-building, and navigation may, therefore, have only limited practical significance at the present time. The following are main sources for such data: 1, 19, 20, 31, 34, 60, 79, 93, 99, 100, 134, 157,

175, 182 (general); 245, 250, 262, 293, 295, 296, 307 (Fiji); 323, 347 (Tonga); 388, 399, 407, 410, 416, 427, 441, 508 (Samoa); 519, 520 (Tokelaus); 530, 534, 535, 538, 540, 546, 550 (Gilberts and Ellices); 581 (Nauru); 595, 596 (Wallis and Horne); 603, 612, 614, 615, 617 (Cooks); 654, 660 (Niue); 676, 709, 738 (Societies); 789, 799 (Tuamotus); 811 (Gambiers); 828 (Australs); 841, 882 (Marquesas); 905, 908, 925 (Polynesian outliers).

Activities could be visualized, under Commission auspices or otherwise, to stimulate greater interest in water-craft of old and new types appropriate to more effective living in such ocean-bound islands: for example, further experimentation perhaps on a regional basis with building and introducing improved types of boats as part of a vocational training programme; encouragement of boat racing and other types of water-sports, perhaps with some inter-island competition (see "Art and Leisure" p. 48). An officially sponsored boat-building programme using local craftsmen and crews has been particularly successful in the Marshall Islands during the post-war period, and it is expected that before long practically all inter-island trade and traffic within that area will be carried in these boats (941, 947).

As regards land transport, which is still mainly by foot trails away from the immediate coastal areas adjacent to the ports, the minor anthropological data available would appear to be of little practical importance other than giving the general economic and social context of trail building and maintenance. Useful anthropological studies could be made, however, of the past or prospective influence of introducing a road-making programme, with its often revolutionary influences on isolated communities, especially as accelerating mobility and change.

Land Tenure and other Property Usages

Most problems of economic welfare and development involve questions relating to the local systems of ownership and use of land and other valued resources. Property customs have always been given close attention by anthropologists as being basic to economic and social organization and to the legal aspect of culture generally. The standard ethnographic surveys for this area contain usually detailed analysis of the traditional land tenure systems and of usages regarding personal property. Furthermore, some attention has been given to adjustments in property concepts and practices which have occurred in the modern period, as through new commercial values placed on land and its produce, and some conversion of indigenous type titles to Western-type titles.

Keesing (105, chapter VI) has given a general survey of the land tenure situation and problems in post-white times, including the impact of varying official policies. He and others have stressed the need for understanding local ideologies surrounding "ownership": the often complex authority rights, typically bound up with the local chieftainship system; the usehold rights (also frequently complex) of those actually occupying landholdings; the seeming paradoxes of multiple or "collective" interests in property combined usually with careful definition of the individual interests involved; and the application of rights to marine resources (lagoon, reef, and adjoining ocean) as well as the conventional land resources. The following are main anthropological references: 2, 18, 95, 105, 108 (general); 204, 205, 214, 221, 254, 277, 294, 295, 298 (Fiji); 323, 342, 345, 361, 372 (Tonga); 388, 396, 404, 427, 438, 441, 457, 482 (Samoa); 519, 520 (Tokelaus); 528, 546, 550 (Gilberts and Ellices); 581, 591 (Nauru); 595, 596 (Wallis and Horne); 603, 614, 615, 616 (Cooks); 660, 662 (Niue); 670, 691, 708, 716 (Societies); 789, 800 (Tuamotus); 811 (Mangareva); 828 (Australs); 871, 882, 892 (Marquesas); 908, 920, 925 (Polynesian outliers).

Fortunately for welfare, this zone of the Pacific does not have traditional types of landlord-tenant relationships such as have produced serious agrarian problems in many western Pacific areas. But some tendency now shows for the older authority rights to metamorphose into tenancy systems. Furthermore, increased value placed on land, together with other factors involved in economic and social change, have led in most territories to extensive land title disputes often calling for court adjudication. Among further matters which may enter into the modern situation are shifts in customs of inheritance, problems associated with leasing and alienation, and sometimes dubious attempts by governments to define and record the indigenous rights in terms of Western law.

Anthropologists have offered scattered comments on such modern problems, but much more remains to be done in investigating typical contemporary situations, particularly in relation to the practical issues which emerge in connexion with developmental planning.

This type of research is in some respects markedly of local significance, because of the great differences in property customs from area to area, and for this reason it might be mainly referred to the Government concerned and to private institutions and scholars. But much of the local experience also has regional significance, as involving principles and policies with wider potential application. From the Commission's viewpoint, some land tenure problems may also arise directly in connexion with its agricultural, marine, forestry, community development, or other projects, and here anthropological workers might be drawn in. Studies on property tenure have been particularly emphasized in the collateral area of American Micronesia in the post-war period (932, 941, 945, 947), and have a long and important history of experimentation among the Polynesian Maoris and Hawaiians (933, 934, 939, 940, 948).

Labour

Anthropologists have discussed considerably the work habits of these peoples in terms of such dimensions as organization, leadership, rhythms, and incentives. They have also brought out the usually strong contrasts between these habits and the concepts of work characteristic of Western communities, with their emphasis on individual achievement, money rewards, and clock and calendar rhythms. The myth of the "lazy," "incompetent," or "unenterprising" native has been effectively exploded through careful examination of labour in its local settings. Economists can profitably take note of anthropological discussions on why Polynesians have usually been unwilling to enter into the work setting of Western enterprises such as the unskilled labour required for plantations and mines; also of the conditions under which they actually do work nowadays in many forms of employment.

Perhaps the most useful sources for such materials are the Beagleholes' Pangai village study (323), Firth's Tikopia (907, 908), several works by Keesing (105, 108, 438), the studies by Geddes and Quain of Fijian villages (221, 277), and Thompson's Lau study (295, 298). Other main sources are: 78, 106, 137, 166 (general); 205, 217, 221, 246, 258, 277, 289, 295 (Fiji); 323, 345 (Tonga); 388, 404, 427, 430, 438, 441, 455, 456, 458, 475 (Samoa); 520 (Tokelaus); 533, 534, 540, 546, 548, 550, 557, 558, 566 (Gilberts and Ellices); 580, 581, 588, 591 (Nauru); 595, 596, 601 (Wallis and Horne); 603, 606, 608, 614, 615,

617, 620 (Cooks); 660, 661 (Niue); 678, 681, 691, 709, 737 (Societies); 784, 789, 790 (Tuamotus); 811 (Gambiers); 828 (Australs); 871, 882, 892 (Marquesas); 907, 908, 915, 925 (Polynesian outliers).

The labour factor is obviously one of the key matters relating to future expansion of economic activities, including any accelerated programme of technical assistance. Administrators are well aware, furthermore, that shortages of wage labour exist in practically every territory. Unless they are prepared to recruit or admit Asiatic labourers, as has often been done in the past but is now nearly everywhere frowned on, islanders must be motivated to engage in more diversified and productive activities. Questions arise, for example, as to how the usually low efficiency of existing hand labour can be improved, how far mechanization is feasible and desirable, how modern forms of labour organization may be penetrating, as in the Cook Islands today.

Such work problems, involving changes in local usage, can be evaluated with profit by anthropological workers, co-operating where necessary with economists and other experts who have stakes in such studies. Though in some respects the needs are local only, any studies would clearly have regional implications. One or more pilot surveys by anthropologists of present-day work habits in carefully selected settings, and of possibilities for modifying such habits in the direction of more effective productivity, could well be given high priority by the Commission. The settings chosen might include the labour situation under indigenous community conditions in a region of rapid population growth, and among workers outside their traditional groups. Studies of this kind could either form a separate category in the work programme or be ancillary to some wider projects in the economic or social development field.

"Low" Island Development and Welfare

This is another topic concerned with all three fields of the Commission's work: economic development, in terms of the possibilities and limitations of local resources and other problems associated with both subsistence and commercial aspects of economic development; social development, in terms of community, educational, and other aspects of population welfare; and health, as regards securing adequate nutrition, water supply, disposal of waste, and good health generally. It will, however, be convenient to include a general discussion of this important problem here, while recognizing that most of the other categories of analysis also apply significantly to welfare and development on such low islands.

Earlier, low and small islands were "typed" as categories I, II, and III (see "Adjustment to the Island Habitats"). From the anthropological aspect a surprisingly extensive amount of information is available, as most of the small inhabited islands have been surveyed by Bishop Museum personnel or other research workers. Outstanding studies of the often remarkable utilization of their land and sea resources are the following: 245, 295, 296, 520, 546, 550, 581, 595, 596, 603, 614, 615, 789, 907, 925. Extensive collateral surveys are also available for the Marshalls and low islands of the Carolines, made by American scholars since the war, e.g., 935, 942, 943, 946, 947. Reports of anthropologists included in two recent U.S. Pacific Science Board scientific teams studying low islands, one working on Arno atoll in the Marshalls (1950, 1951), the other on Onotoa in the Gilberts (1951), will be most important as representing collaborative work with other scientists.

A striking feature emphasized by anthropological studies is the considerable variability in low island types and resources: some, for example, are very young and low atolls with little fertile land for cultivation and maximum dependence by their populations on marine resources. At the other extreme are raised coral pancakes without barrier reefs and less dependence on the sea; some, especially in the central and western Pacific, have higher rainfall or richer soil structure and can grow more varied agricultural products than others such as the relatively barren northern Cooks and many of the Tuamotus in the eastern Pacific. Low islands may also have some minor volcanic outcropping to give a greater diversification in products.

These variables would need to be taken into account in choosing significant sites for further studies. An investigation, no matter how thorough, of one island or island type only would have limited and unsure application to other areas. It would also be wise to select, if possible, islands for which extensive anthropological and other scientific data are already available rather than having to begin from meagre information.

Welfare and development problems on small islands become particularly serious where modern tendencies to population increase become strongly operative (see "Population Numbers and Trends", p. 12). The often stark limits of local resources show in choices, perhaps, as to how far the available coconut crop can be used for commercial copra production without lowering the nutritional standards. Already migration has set in strongly from some of the low islands to the higher island centres (see "Urban Development" p. 52), and even to the metropolitan countries, and this will doubtless expand. The question has sometimes been raised by outsiders as to whether the often scanty number of families occupying an isolated low island should not be bodily removed and resettled elsewhere. But ties of the low islanders with their ancestral habitats appear to be strong, and forcible removal is out of line with modern concepts of welfare. The fostering of such "colonies" at the centres of employment and greater opportunity appears to offer an important safety valve for small island development. Perhaps, indeed, in the more distant future, the pull of these colonies may lead to the voluntary abandonment of many of the very small outer islands, with advantage to the peoples and administrations concerned. Meantime the tasks of fostering their maximum development in terms both of subsistence and of commercial benefits to the population provide an outstanding challenge.

Reference to more specific economic problems is covered by other sections ("Agriculture," "Marine Products" etc.). From the anthropological viewpoint the available data can be greatly strengthened by sharper formulation of the problems to which attention could be given in the future. Such issues as population increase, any current changes in the utilization of resources such as the introduction of new crops or livestock, the relation of production to the existing social system, penetration of the commercial economy, and other trends of modern acculturation generally, would be directly of concern to the anthropologist working alone or as part of a larger team. He would also be able to help in exploring the context of other problems with which he is technically less familiar, such as improvement of water supply, sanitation, pest control, or the experimental introduction of new production methods. Studies of low island conditions and problems have, of course, been given top priority already in the Commission's programme.

The Independent Smallholder

How far is smallholding likely to be an effective solution to economic and social problems? This question tends to be most important currently as regards population elements of mixed ancestry, especially for those who aspire to European status, and to immigrant settlers such as the Indian farmers of Fiji. But it is also of increasing significance among the indigenous peoples as they become more educated and aware of Western patterns of rural settlement.

Anthropological studies show reasonably fully the traditional types of settlement, varying from tightly knit village communities to small hamlets and occasionally scattered out farmsteads (see "Patterns of Settlement" p. 40). How a people used to spreading out could adapt relatively easily to smallholding is well illustrated in the case of Tonga. Here the Government for many years permitted every male Tongan at the age of sixteen to apply for an agricultural allotment, provided planting is done, as well as a town lot. The background and operation of this scheme is described in 323, 345, 372. The holder has usehold rights only, and a small rental is paid, as the title remains with the Crown or a hereditary estate owner; the system is an outgrowth of the older Tongan land customs. Even so, problems have arisen because many Tongans are failing to exercise these land rights. Smallholding is also to quite an extent characteristic of Tahiti.

For the islander who has back of him a strong tradition of group living, whether in villages or hamlets, Western-style proprietorship calls for a more or less sharp break with established custom, and few have essayed a shift in this direction except around the urban centres. Not only would social pressures and perhaps local systems of land tenure militate against it, but also little advantage would be gained without accessibility to commercial-type services and markets. Even in Samoa, where Europeans and especially nowadays part-Samoans depend mainly outside the town centres on smallholding, very few of the Samoans have broken with village living. Here studies are available of the family and community system which exercises such a hold (see under "Social Systems"). Though local customs of owning and using property may take on a greater flavour of Western usages as now representing potential money value, and transfer of rights may involve some buying and selling, the group interests show few signs of being transmuted into individual interests.

The most interesting laboratory, undoubtedly, in relation to this general problem is Fiji. Considerable information is already available in governmental sources, supplemented by a modicum of anthropological analysis, e.g., 197, 204, 205, 244, 253, 271. Here the great majority of the 135,000 Indians are rural smallholders, also many of the part-Europeans, and a small but increasing number of ambitious and usually more educated Fijians who elect to leave their villages and establish individual and family farms. In terms of regional significance, the last group is especially important, and could profitably be made the subject of a special study, under the auspices of the Commission or otherwise. The Government has carried out for more than two decades various schemes for the settlement of Fijian smallholders, not only giving special training and other technical aid, but also making provision for lands to become available outside the village holdings and for monetary payments to be made to the home community in lieu of "communal" services. A policy balance has had to be maintained here between encouraging and improving the village system for those electing to live still in traditional style communities, as for example through the co-operative society movement now making headway, and giving scope for the development of individualism as expressed in such Western style farming pursuits. It would be particularly interesting to have assessed the degree to which the increasing tendency toward smallholding among Fijians is conditioned by such factors as the size of the islands, the availability of transport and of markets for products, vocational training, and the nature of official policies, particularly in making suitable lands available under individual title; the extent of success or of failure among such settlers, and the repercussions upon the home communities. A "Fijian Development Fund", created in 1951, has important potentialities for the economic future, both for those Fijians who elect to try smallholding and for those who prefer to remain within organized groups.

Another needed type of study for some territories relates to the position of those part-islanders who elect to settle as smallholders. The economic position of this group has been particularly crucial to date in Western Samoa, where the experience of the Aleisa settlement scheme for part-Samoans would be especially relevant. In Fiji, too, there are several part-Fijian farming groups which could profitably be studied. Some more detailed surveys of Indian or Chinese smallholders in the islands would also have facets of regional as well as of local significance. It goes without saying that any such investigations undertaken in their anthropological aspects would require close co-operation between the workers concerned and economic specialists. The closely related topic of "Urban Development" is dealt with in chapter III.

III

SOCIAL DEVELOPMENT

THIS category covers such matters as population distribution and movement, community organization, housing, family and class systems,
ideologies, recreation and education. It inevitably overlaps in many
respects that of economic development, and to a lesser degree that
of health. The basic topic of "Population Numbers and Trends,"
treated in the last chapter, might, for example, have been discussed
at least equally well under this heading, because of the intimate
relation of fertility and mortality, and of age and sex differentiation,
to family and community organization and ideologies; also because
changes in social conditions and values, including modern types of
education, have exercised such a profound influence on population
trends.

Because social problems are not so often sharply focused and of
direct regional significance as those in economic and health fields,
a larger proportion of the items listed appear to be more suited to
research by private institutions and scholars than by the Commission,
e.g., household order, leadership systems, religion. Yet basic knowledge
of social settings must form an essential backdrop for the adequate
study of virtually all other problems, so that such materials have their
practical importance and recording them should be given every
encouragement.

Education

A general survey, with bibliography, of education in Polynesia
has been prepared by Marie Keesing (112). Further overall analyses of
the problems involved are offered in the report of a Seminar-Conference on "Education in Pacific Countries" held in 1936 at the University of Hawaii jointly by that institution and Yale University (104),
and in Keesing (105, chapter XII).

Anthropologists have contributed important materials on child
rearing and training in such societies. They cover with varying
effectiveness the indigenous background of education; learning and
training methods, and more generally the nature of personality

development in the group concerned. Among the most notable works are those by the Beagleholes for Tonga and Pukapuka (Cook Islands), and collaterally in Hawaii and for the New Zealand Maori (322, 323, 605, 606, 933, 934); Buck for Samoa (389); Firth for Tikopia (907); Hogbin for Ongtong Java (912, 917); Linton for the Marquesas (883); Mead for Samoa (136, 138, 455, 456); Geddes and Quain for Fiji (221, 277); Thompson for the Laus and collaterally for Guam (295, 296, 949), and Wedgwood for Nauru (591).

Materials of this kind are particularly significant for understanding the child in terms of the pre-school setting, the wider social and educational context from which the older children come to school, and the needs and opportunities which the adult will have in the post-school years. Such works as those referred to show clearly that indigenous education, though characteristically informal and based on "learning by doing," is not haphazard. Training is also occasionally institutionalized to a marked degree as in instruction for children of the aristocracies, and "apprenticeship" in arts and crafts. More study is needed, however, of such indigenous systems of education, and of the settings in which children are reared.

The old-time training of the youth involved a less complicated problem than that of today, because the task was essentially to initiate children to already established patterns of life. Now the latter are greatly changed and in a considerable state of flux, while the indigenous societies are in a dynamic state as regards population numbers, interpenetrated by peoples of radically different cultures, and pressed upon increasingly by the larger world of twentieth century affairs. This is justification, in spite of some lingering sentimental ideas to the contrary, for intruding the modern institution of the school with its more systematic learning and professional personnel for instruction, as offering possibilities of guidance and control. It also justifies special enterprises such as adult education, stimulation of literacy, provision of literature suitable for village use, and experimentation with audio-visual aids, all of which are of interest to the Commission.

Anthropologists have had less to say on modern schooling. But they have commented in scattered works on the various alternatives of policy involved, such as the place to be given in a curriculum to local knowledge, hand-crafts, and other matters arising out of the indigenous setting; the question of how far the vernacular language should be used; the problems of advanced education and vocational and professional training, considered in terms of the local needs and opportunities; and the alternatives of government versus private (including mission) control of education. Some interesting materials relating to the experimental establishment of a school for sons of American Samoan chiefs, the Barstow Memorial "Feleti" School, now replaced by a general high school, are found in 379, 387, 415, 459. More directly in the anthropological tradition are some important discussions of the sharp contrasts between the traditional forms and expectations of personality development and those likely to be emphasized in the Western-type school programme; also of the resulting inconsistencies and insecurities generated in many of the younger people in their efforts to master two very different worlds of thought and custom. In addition to the above citations, especially works by the Beagleholes, Buck, the Keesings, Mead, and Thompson, the following references are particularly useful: 68, 78, 82, 111, 156 (general); 220, 228, 229, 232, 265, 284 (Fiji); 344, 372 (Tonga); 387, 403, 409, 412, 437, 438, 477, 497, 513 (Samoa); 536, 556, 558 (Gilberts and Ellices); 614, 615, 616, 635 (Cooks); 789, 790 (Tuamotus); 871 (Marquesas).

The following are among the fields in which social anthropologists can continue to contribute significantly:

(a) The pre-school background of young children, including indigenous-style training, and the social context within which early child-rearing is carried on. This appears to be particularly appropriate for study by private institutions and scholars rather than by the Commission because of its scientific emphasis and lack of practical problem focus.

(b) Closely related to the above, the local systems of personality development and of valued adult personality (character) structure toward which the indigenous society directs each generation, and their relation to the usages and objectives of Western-type schooling. This kind of study also seems primarily suited to the more academic approach, not least of all because it is somewhat controversial in terms of various "schools" in social anthropology, and is still largely at an experimental stage of formulation. But its importance cannot be questioned.

(c) The methods and content of school curricula, especially for elementary schools in different types of communities from isolated village schools to urban groups. An anthropologist, in association with educators, can be of help in assessing how far local methods of teaching and subject-matter appear suited to pupil needs, including the desirable balance between indigenous and Western elements. This material, and also the principles involved, would be in many respects of regional as well as of local concern. Included here could be the matter of preparing school texts, some of which might well be developed for the region as a whole or for schools in tropical countries fairly generally, as with simple materials on geography, agriculture, fishing, housing, and home science, and the basic matter of teaching English or French.

(d) More advanced instruction, including vocational training. Here the anthropological approach may be particularly useful, conjoined with that of administrators, health experts, and others, in giving a more realistic assessment of needs and opportunities within the local settings. The Commission might well give high priority to several sample surveys of vocational needs and outlets in the different types of community setting, e.g., small and low islands; isolated zones of larger islands; urban centres. The controversial question as to how far advanced education in such areas is to be measured wholly against yardsticks of narrowly vocational outlets could be included in the sphere of reference here. So, too, could the important question of differential instruction for boys and for girls, including significant training in home science for the latter.

(e) The language problem in schools and otherwise could profitably be put in part into the hands of anthropologists for further study. Controversies over whether to use the vernacular (or a local *lingua franca*), or a Western language, have become increasingly tempered by a realization that island groups are becoming, under the self-education of necessity, bilingual or even multi-lingual. There are two rather different approaches involved here. One is that of the trained linguist, who may be needed where work has to be done on improving orthographies or otherwise handling special linguistic techniques. The other is that of the social anthropologist who can study language needs and trends in their wider cultural setting. The Commission might follow up its initial project on language[1] by sponsoring one or more pilot studies of the language situation in

[1] The report on this project by Dr. A. Capell is shortly to be published for the Commission by the Oxford University Press.

D

relation to school policies, with special attention to bilingualism, though this might have less priority here than in the more complex linguistic situations in the adjacent Melanesian areas.

(f) The social context of mass literacy, audio-visual activities, and adult education in general. It would be well, in advancing further investigations in these fields, to have anthropological advice, and to launch any special anthropological studies which may seem profitable here. Where the trained expert in these educational fields is likely to have the approach of one looking into the society from outside for want of familiarity with local settings, an anthropological worker, as a specialist on getting the inside view, could be of great help in suggesting the most profitable lines of contact, assessing the impact of particular experiments, and following up results to judge their permanence. This could be done, for example, as regards the important recent experiments in broadcasting to Western Samoan villages. In any more intensive pilot experiments in these fields, therefore, the Commission would do well to try to get anthropological representation on the team concerned.

(g) Educational problems connected with non-indigenous groups, such as colonies of islanders from the outer areas living at port centres, part-islanders, or Asian settlers. Here, equally, the contexts of custom could be studied profitably. These problems have some regional as well as local significance. The numerical size of such groups is usually increasing and the proportion of sub-adults is typically large. The educational problems involved are correspondingly expanding. One dimension which could profit by anthropological study is that of segregated versus non-segregated schooling, on which official and also mission policies differ in the South Pacific Territories.

Patterns of Settlement

For many of the projects in which the Commission is interested, the distribution of local population and types of community living have importance. The anthropological literature generally describes these for earlier days, though less fully as they are today except in a relatively few studies. The following are the most relevant sources: 31, 105, 106 (general); 221, 224, 245, 277, 295, 296 (Fiji); 323, 342, 345 (Tonga); 427, 438, 441, 455 (Samoa); 519, 520 (Tokelaus); 534, 540, 565 (Gilberts and Ellices); 581, 582, 591 (Nauru); 595, 596 (Wallis and Horne); 603, 614, 615, 616, 620 (Cooks); 660, 661 (Niue); 670, 698, 708, 716 (Societies); 767, 786, 787, 789 (Tuamotus); 811 (Gambiers); 828 (Australs); 855, 871, 882, 892 (Marquesas); 907, 921, 925, 930 (Polynesian outliers).

These peoples have varied from zone to zone as to whether their habitat conditions and their cultural preferences have led them to aggregate in villages, in smaller hamlets, or in scattered homesteads. Most Polynesians, and also the Fijians, have occupied closely knit villages, with up to perhaps four hundred persons in the largest communities under aboriginal conditions, and now occasionally more than that number. But some Polynesians, and also most Micronesians, have scattered out in hamlets, or even, as in Hawaii and Tonga if early records are to be believed, frequently in family "farmsteads." In modern days some minor tendencies have shown toward greater scattering, made more possible under conditions of peace, and with the impetus of new economic and other stimulation. But for the most part the peoples have, if anything, consolidated somewhat further under mission and other influences. The newest element in the modern scene is the development of urban centres at a few key points, containing the bulk of the immigrant populations, and drawing in increasing numbers of islanders from the outer areas (see "Urban Development" p. 52).

So-called "community" studies have become quite important in modern social anthropology. Though much general material exists in the literature, only a few detailed surveys of a contemporary community are so far available even for the whole region: the Beagleholes' monograph on Pangai village in Tonga (323), studies by Geddes and Quain on two Fijian villages (220, 221, 277), and Firth's Tikopia materials (907); Mead's study of Samoan adolescent girls on Ta'u approximates to another (455).

Such documents do not ordinarily have the sharp practical focus to which the Commission gives priority in its work programme. Yet it seems highly desirable to encourage such research by private institutions and scholars in order to give increasingly authentic background materials for other studies. In the case of any Commission project using the comprehensive approach now often called "Community Development" such a study or its equivalent in detailed, on-the-spot observation would be essential. The same is true where more specific problems relating to group activities and services within a community are of concern: e.g., schooling as referred to above, the improvement of sanitation or water supplies, the installation of radio, of power facilities, or a sawmill. Already in several Territories, for instance, life in some villages has been markedly changed by the availability of electric light and power either from the town services or locally generated. In many aspects of technical development the local community is likely to be the most important unit, as in the activities of co-operatives.

Housing

The traditional styles of house structure are usually described in great detail, with accompanying diagrams, in the anthropological literature. Also revealed is a surprising amount of adaptation in housing which has taken place in post-white times e.g., the spread of Tahitian architecture in eastern Polynesia, particularly as a concomitant of mission work; the use of piles for house foundations in several places; some use of corrugated iron for roofing. But the general trends are conservative; for example, the persistence of house shapes, stone platform foundations where these were customary, leaf roofing and perhaps leaf walls, the cooking shed nearly always a separate structure, sleeping usually on floor mats. The well-known house-builders' guilds of Samoa present perhaps the extreme of conservatism. The following are main sources: 22, 72, 178 (general); 221, 246, 277, 295, 296 (Fiji); 323, 352 (Tonga); 385, 388, 427, 430, 441 (Samoa); 519, 520 (Tokelaus); 531, 534, 546, 550, 565 (Gilberts and Ellices); 581 (Nauru); 595, 596 (Wallis and Horne); 603, 612, 614, 615, 617 (Cooks); 674, 698, 709 (Societies); 789 (Tuamotus); 811 (Gambiers); 828 (Australs); 847, 856, 871, 882, 900 (Marquesas); 907, 925 (Polynesian outliers).

Problems of housing improvement have to be visualized mainly within the limitations of existing local materials, work habits, and social customs. Unless the government concerned is willing to give subsidies, any imported building materials and equipment for a typical home must be very cheap and small in quantity, e.g., piping, wire meshing or glass may be prohibitive in terms of local money income standards. Though some *élite* families may nowadays own quite elaborate houses, perhaps of European style, any aspirations on the part of the mass of the people toward such housing other than perhaps in the urban centres are likely to be, for the present, unrealistic.

This does not mean that housing cannot be improved. Surveys would be worth-while, if not already made by the authorities concerned, to ascertain how local house styles could be adapted for better lighting, sanitation, preservation and usability. Installation of windows where custom does not allow for or permit them is an example of a problem needing further study. If, as yet, tradition against such an overt change remains too strong, it might be possible to introduce some compromise adaptation such as vents in the walls to allow better air circulation, once the leaders and people are convinced of the health benefits which would accrue. Some house styles might have porches added with advantage; cooking houses might be made more sanitary; simple safes with wire coverings might possibly be made fashionable. The writer found village people particularly worried by the problems of preservation and repair of houses made of the traditional materials, now that commercialism is penetrating to the point where such materials, and even services relating to house building, may have to be paid for. Here reasonably priced materials for making structures insect-resistant, and possibly a transparent plastic spray which could be coated over a whole house to add to its life, might be answers which an experimental "technical assistance" team could work out, affecting the lives not only of these islanders but of millions of people like them elsewhere.

Housing problems would lend themselves particularly well to experiments in dissemination of useful ideas from one group to another, as through slides, simple diagrams, and text materials. All these matters involve the question of ideologies and incentives as well as of opportunities and practical demonstrations, especially if any experimental housing improvements are to become permanent. Here the social anthropologist can be of special aid, and the Commission's project relating to housing improvement will doubtless take account of this approach.

Social Systems

Anthropologists have always laid great stress on the analysis of social systems: community and household organization, kinship, age, sex, and class distinctions, leadership, and social order. For most of these ethnic groups the traditional systems have been described in detail; see especially: 18, 40, 68, 75, 92, 94, 95, 121, 125, 126, 136, 139, 140, 141, 145, 152, 167, 181, 184, 186, 187 (general); 198, 199, 202,

217, 220, 221, 224, 238, 239, 245, 248, 251, 255, 256, 257, 258, 262, 268, 272, 277, 279, 289, 295, 296, 300 (Fiji); 323, 337, 338, 345 (Tonga); 391, 392, 393, 394, 396, 400, 401, 414, 427, 428, 433, 438, 439, 441, 447, 455, 456, 457, 458, 467, 471, 482, 483, 487, 504, 506, 509 (Samoa); 519, 520 (Tokelaus); 534, 536, 546, 558, 559, 560, 570 (Gilberts and Ellices); 581, 582, 591 (Nauru); 595, 596 (Wallis and Horne); 603, 605, 614, 615, 616, 619, 635, 639, 641, 642 (Cooks); 660 (Niue); 663, 672, 673, 681, 692, 708, 713, 716, 719, 727, 728, 737, 745, 751 (Societies); 766, 767, 768, 782, 789 (Tuamotus); 811, 818, 822, 823, 824 (Gambiers); 828, 839 (Australs); 855, 871, 883, 892, 897, 898 (Marquesas); 907, 909, 912, 914, 915, 916, 918, 920, 925 (Polynesian outliers).

Materials showing modern changes in social systems and conditions as they exist today are more sporadic. But there is considerable information in the works cited above, and several useful studies are focused directly on this approach, notably the Beagleholes' Pangai village for Tonga (323); the Fiji village studies by Geddes and by Quain (220, 221, 277); Keesing's general summaries and Samoa studies (105, 106, 438, 439); Mead's *Coming of Age in Samoa* (455), and Thompson's survey of contemporary Lau (295).

An understanding of the present-day island societies must underlie much of the Commission's work programme, and it comes particularly to the fore in such projects as community development, economic studies where understanding of local leadership and work organization is involved, mass education, and disease prevention. This aspect of cultural analysis has been particularly stressed in recent studies of American Micronesia (these are summarized in 941; more specific examples are 931, 932, 944, 947, 950). In general, however, such research, which requires in many respects the trained techniques of modern social anthropology[2] if the results are to be more than amateur and casual observations, does not have a sharply practical character. One important and increasingly used approach so far almost completely lacking in studies of the area is the recording *in extenso* of life histories as a means of revealing development and participation within such societies.

These social systems have been undergoing a selective process of change ever since the Europeans arrived, in some respects voluntarily,

[2] See, for example, Lowie, R. H., *Social Organization*, New York, 1948; Murdock, G.P., *Social Structure*, New York, 1949; Lévy-Strauss, C., *Les Structures Elémentaires de la Parenté*, Paris, 1949; Firth, R., *Elements of Social Organization*, London, 1951; Radcliffe-Brown, A. R., "The Study of Kinship Systems", *R.A.I.J.*, 71, 2.

and in others under mission and government pressures. But the general emphasis is still to the conservative side. Such peoples do not change drastically their intimate social habits such as those of sex, family behaviour, etiquette, and community security, or their socio-political groupings and *élites*, except under extreme acculturation needs or pressures. Even among those living in the urban centres and among the immigrant groups they tend to continue quite strongly. Governments today are rightly conservative, too, about taking any arbitrary steps which interfere in anything but essential matters with self-motivated development, whether in the directions of change or of resistance to change.

If this viewpoint is accepted, it would seem that further studies of the island social systems, important as they are, could for the most part be done best by private institutions and scholars rather than directly within the Commission's developing work programme. This does not rule out the possibility of the Commission giving full encouragement toward much needed elaboration of such studies. Furthermore, special matters such as those relating to community development, the organization of economic activity, or to health improvement, will undoubtedly enter into Commission projects, as pointed out above.

One very practical problem here relates to the development of "community centres." Many of these island societies have had special localities for group assemblages and other social and ceremonial activities: e.g., a village "square"; "men's houses" or other types of assembly halls; chiefs' guest houses. The customs connected with them may still be active, but in many communities they have fallen considerably into obsolescence, perhaps with the decline of the old religion, or they may afford centres for men's activities only. Nowadays a government office, schoolhouse or church may serve something of the function of a community centre. Anthropological studies in several areas (934, 940, 948) have revealed the damage to group morale and identity that may come about where any such traditional social centre falls into disuse, and by contrast the great social and psychological benefits that accrue from having such a rallying point where the people may gather for serious consultation and for play. The ideal centre might include both outdoor and indoor meeting places, a platform stage and appropriate seating accommodations, kitchen space, sports areas and equipment, and perhaps work space for hand-crafts. Studies by anthropologists of the existing social facilities in selected communities and of possible means for improvement should be made a high priority Commission project.

Ideology and Religion

Much of what has been said in the previous chapter applies directly here. Documentation of the old bodies of knowledge, religion, folk-lore, and life viewpoints ("philosophies") are elaborated in the litera-ture, so far as they could be known through records and by questioning informants in later days, with folklore particularly emphasized. Anthropological interpretation of modern changes in these aspects of culture, though occasionally perhaps over-sentimental, is also quite extensive.

A general review and summary of the sources on religion and mission work is given by Keesing (105, chapter XI), while a vivid interpretation of the acculturative processes has been made, mainly from Cook Island materials, by Buck (32). Luomala has summarized the considerable contributions of missionary workers to religious and other anthropological studies, and gives a comprehensive biblio-graphy (129). The following are other main sources on ideology and religion (exclusive of folklore materials which are listed separately in the final paragraphs of this section): 29, 30, 47, 68, 75, 76, 78, 89, 91, 97, 120, 133, 148, 181, 185, 186 (general); 191, 200, 203, 213, 221, 225, 240, 242, 245, 246, 259, 262, 266, 266a, 274, 276, 277, 278, 279, 287, 289, 295, 296, 297, 299 (Fiji); 323, 329, 330, 333, 333a, 334, 335, 336, 345 (Tonga); 376, 390, 427, 438, 441, 447, 455, 472, 484, 490, 493, 507, 509 (Samoa); 519, 520 (Tokelaus); 534, 539, 546 (Gilberts and Ellices); 581, 591 (Nauru); 595, 596 (Wallis and Horne); 603, 606, 614, 615, 616, 624, 625, 630, 633, 634, 642 (Cooks); 659, 660 (Niue); 698, 700, 708, 716, 719, 745, 759 (Societies); 774, 781, 782, 785, 788, 789, 790, 796, 801, 805, 806 (Tuamotus); 811, 817, 818, 821, 826 (Gambiers); 828, 830 (Australs); 849, 855, 856, 859, 860, 871, 883, 890, 892, 898 (Marquesas); 906, 907, 909, 913, 919, 924, 925 (Poly-nesian outliers).

Of particular interest to anthropologists have been so-called "nativistic" or "adjustment" movements among various groups, nearly always with a strong religious character. Here peoples caught in the insecurities of change and of outside pressure have followed cult-leaders who purport to have new revelations of "truth." These latter are based nearly always in part on reformulations of the old faiths no longer adequate, and in part on Christian ideas which, taken as a whole, often seem too alien. Such movements have been widely reported from comparable frontier areas the world over. The known materials for this island region are summarized in Keesing (105, pp. 238); other main references are in 32, 110, 200, 277, 295, 365, 402, 438, 495, 727, 892, 933, 934, 939, 940, 948.

Social anthropologists have been emphasizing over the last decade, especially in the United States, the study of what are often called the "value systems" inherent in different cultures, or (looked at from other slants) the "ideologies," "goal systems," "master-ideas," "themes," "character traits," or whatever else particular students may choose to call the basic assumptions, interpretations, and evaluations of life as expressed in those cultures. The practical man might at first consider such investigations remote from his problems. But social scientists now are realizing that it is to these levels of motivation that the man of action must somehow penetrate if he wishes to tap the incentives and "emotional mainsprings" of the people concerned.

The successful administrator in a Pacific Island setting, just as the successful advertising expert or political leader at home, knows his people well enough in the rough, through empirical experience, to take account in large measure of these basic sets. In the long term view, careful scientific studies of the "character" of these island peoples may be of very great value. Today they are somewhat controversial, receiving different stress by various anthropological and psychological schools and scholars; these controversies centre less, however, upon their worth than on the difficulties of getting precise tools for analysis and interpretation of these levels of behaviour. So far, the most important literature in this field is for cultures outside this island area, e.g., Benedict, R., *The Chrysanthemum and the Sword* (Japan); Du Bois, C., *People of Alor* (Indonesia); Kardiner, A., *Psychological Frontiers of Society*; Kluckhohn, C. and Leighton, D., *The Navaho*; Beaglehole, E. and P., *Some Modern Maoris*; and particularly now quite numerous technical papers in the scientific literature, some including careful critiques of such pioneering and experimental works. For the area being considered, only a few studies are yet available from these view-points, notably some of the Beagleholes' Tongan and Cook Island materials (322, 323, 603-606); Linton on the Marquesas (883); Mead

48   SOCIAL ANTHROPOLOGY IN POLYNESIA

on Samoa (136, 138, 455, 456); Quain's Fijian village (277), and Thompson on the Lau islands in Fiji (295, 298). A paper presented at the Seventh Pacific Science Congress by Keesing (110) emphasizes the great potential importance to administration of such studies, revealing the complexities involved when peoples with different value-systems and other "character" sets are having to adjust themselves to one another, and to the larger world situation.

One special source for understanding the basic ideologies of such peoples is the folklore which they consider worth remembering and passing down generation by generation: myth materials which offer primary explanations of life problems and also validations of the cultural solutions which have been worked out; tales of gods and heroes; stories with a moral core or giving pleasure; "historical" narratives; proverbs, and so on. Such bodies of oral lore have special importance to peoples who have lacked writing until recently. Yet they have tended to die out, especially where missions have considered their content "heathen." Now, however, it is becoming recognized that preserving these old traditions can have some importance in giving peoples caught in the cross-currents of modern contacts a stabilizing sense of pride and of continuity with the past. Educators have also found use for folklore materials in school work, though, as in Samoa, the introduction of sacred elements or of tales which glorify some families and communities at the expense of others can cause trouble. In the local setting the conservation of folklore helps to round out leisure activities such as are referred to in the next section. The following are the main sources: 3, 16, 47, 61, 86, 128, 130, 131, 132, 133, 150 (general); 201, 215, 222, 274, 276, 277, 286 (Fiji); 339, 343, 358, 359 (Tonga); 418, 419, 420, 441, 443, 446, 461, 465, 466, 467, 481, 484, 486, 489, 490, 496 (Samoa); 516, 520 (Tokelaus); 534, 537 (Gilberts and Ellices); 581 (Nauru); 595, 596 (Wallis and Horne); 603, 628, 630, 642, 646, 652 (Cooks); 660, 661 (Niue); 663, 665, 684, 687, 700, 708, 714, 715, 716, 750, 751, 759 (Societies); 765, 766, 768, 769, 770, 781, 802, 807, 808 (Tuamotus); 811 (Gambiers); 828 (Australs); 849, 872 (Marquesas); 925 (Polynesian outliers).

Art and Leisure

This is another category in which anthropologists have recorded extensive data, but which would be of concern for privately sponsored research rather than the Commission, as not involving sharply practical problems. Anthropologists have recorded not only traditional and newer art, music, dancing, sports, and other modes of entertainment and relaxation, but also the important functions of these forms of self-expression in giving personal and group satisfaction and integration.

Important works by Bateson, Greiner, Leenhardt, Linton, and Wingert have reviewed the island art as a whole, mostly with excellent illustrative materials (9, 83, 119, 124, 183). There are also some general surveys, notably by Andersen and Burrows, of music and musical instruments (4, 24, 38, 41, 59). Outstanding regional works in the art field are by Willowdean Handy for the Societies and the Marquesas (711, 877), and von den Steinen for the Marquesas (895), and in music by Burrows for Wallis and Horne, and for the Tuamotus (598, 773), Crampton for Tahiti (689), Densmore for Samoa (408), Elbert and the Handys for the Marquesas (863, 873), Kennedy for Fiji (249), and Roberts for the Societies (746). Several scholars have written special works about sports, games and dances, notably Bunzendahl for the Societies (678), Churchill for Samoa (399), Damm on some general Polynesian sports (54, 55), Firth for Tikopia (904), Heider for Samoa (431), Hocart for Fiji (236), Kennedy for Tonga (349), and Rougier for Fiji (282). Other main references are 56, 60, 95, 98, 102, 105, 168 (general); 206, 221, 225, 251, 268, 270, 276, 277, 286, 292, 295, 296 (Fiji); 323, 331, 345 (Tonga); 419, 421, 427, 430, 434, 438, 439, 440, 441, 447, 450, 451, 455, 457, 486, 508 (Samoa); 519, 520 (Tokelaus); 527, 534, 535 (Gilberts and Ellices); 578, 581, 583, 590, 591 (Nauru); 595, 596 (Wallis and Horne); 603, 606, 611, 614, 615, 616, 621, 634, 649 (Cooks); 660 (Niue); 677, 697, 700, 708, 710, 749 (Societies); 765, 789 (Tuamotus); 811, 825 (Gambiers); 828, 835, 836, 840 (Australs); 845, 854, 864, 871, 874, 875, 882, 893, 894 (Marquesas); 909, 925, 926 (Polynesian outliers).

Modern changes have included everywhere a considerable decline in many traditional activities of this kind, and even the extinction of some. Yet there has also been usually a vigorous acceptance of appreciated European substitutes such as football, cricket, baseball, and (in the town centres) the cinema. Students of culture-change have stressed here the special role of art and sport as giving constructive outlets and reinforcing self-confidence under the difficult conditions so often created. Recent inter-island contests, as with games between representatives of Tonga, Samoa, and Fiji, are also exercising an important educative influence in expanding local horizons. The Commission might consider lending its weight to the initiation of several South Pacific "festivals" to be held annually at strategic centres, starting with the three territories mentioned and others adjacent to them with games, dancing, music, boat-racing, and other appropriate competitions and exhibitions. As with the Caribbean area, this could well provide additionally an important commercial stimulus by attracting tourists to the area.

Co-operative Activities

The interest of the Commission in modern-type "co-operatives," already a subject on which studies are under way, can have as a background some useful references in the anthropological literature as to the extent and nature of co-operative activities already existing among these peoples. Recent field workers, particularly in dealing with economic and social organization, have recorded materials relevant to this topic. A key study by Maude of modern co-operatives in the Gilbert and Ellice Islands is available (557). Keesing presents a general discussion (105), and also information on Samoa (438); Mead analyses the relations of the individual to the group in Samoan society (456), and also has a more general work on co-operation and competition (458); the village studies of the Beagleholes, Geddes and Quain show co-operative enterprises in action (220, 221, 277, 323); and much pertinent material is scattered through the sources listed under "Social Systems" (p. 43).

A pitfall avoided by anthropologists today is to over-simplify the frequently co-operative habits of such peoples. Such vague terms as "communal" or "collective" are particularly under suspicion where they give the impression that individuality merges into the total group for all activities. Persons do act co-operatively as members of various groups, and exercise rights and duties in them, perhaps including the sharing of interests in property: the household, various kinship alignments, neighbourly and friendly associations, the community as a whole, and perhaps district groupings. But personal rights and opportunities are also likely to be carefully defined, so that individuality is not lost. How far the total emphasis, in terms of any local value system (see "Ideology and Religion" p. 46), is upon group participation rather than individual achievement appears to vary considerably. It may well prove, for example, that some of the island societies would accept much more readily a modern co-operative society system for managing their business affairs than others.

An important factor in the development of modern type co-operative activities is the leadership system. Some co-operative schemes which have been tried to date have failed because of inexperienced management, or because officers have favoured their own families or other special interests. In New Zealand, the Maoris in many cases found it wise in setting up group enterprises of modern type to employ competent European managers from outside, not least of all because of these factors. In the islands, supervision for co-operatives has generally been given by governments, with islanders who are more or less trained conducting the local management. Certain difficulties in relations between the traditional type leadership and such new business leadership in more than one area led the First South Pacific Conference to pass a resolution recognizing the "importance of taking all possible steps to avoid risk of conflict." This leadership problem illustrates well how anthropological studies revealing the present-day context of co-operation might be fruitful.

Social Disorganization

Anthropological studies of law and social control in the traditional island societies indicate that rules, though strongly binding, were sometimes broken, evoking sanctions of social and supernatural character including prescribed procedures and punishments. In modern days, however, conformity to rules has been greatly complicated by the fact that the local codes have had superimposed upon them new codes of Western origin. The latter, variously insisted upon by missions and governments, have inevitably been in some respect directly contrary to the indigenous rules. Whichever way the islander has behaved in these matters, therefore, he has been a delinquent.

Other new usages, whether insisted upon by outside dictum or voluntarily accepted, inevitably have had the indirect effect of undermining old authority. Or else, if they had no close relation to the customary setting they might fail to evoke more than erratic conformity or mere lip-service, for want of being related to local values and sanctions. For an individual here and there, such strains become so great that they result in personality breakdowns; such conditions are likely to appear particularly in and around the port areas where cultural conflicts and pressures are most intensive. The fact that anthropologists, as other social scientists, are able to say of such happenings that they are characteristic of societies in times of cultural change does not mitigate the problems involved for the individuals and groups concerned. It may even be more painful to bear the consequences of community or family disapproval because of non-conformity than to be punished by an official court or jail.

This context of social disorganization and delinquency needs more detailed investigation than it has been given to date, though again it seems a subject more for private than for Commission research. Among extant studies particularly bearing on it are those by the Beagleholes (322, 323, 603-606); Buck (32); Hogbin (920); Keesing (105, 110); Mead (455); Thompson (295); and Wedgwood (591); there are also scattered references, particularly in the works cited under "Social Systems" p. 43). In the next section on "Urban Development" reference is made to conditions in the towns which may particularly foster social disorganization; but study is also needed of how these problems occur under village conditions. It need hardly be said that group pressures toward conformity with tradition, and suspicions of outside interference, may at times provide major road blocks in the way of desirable change and development. Better understanding of these forces is, therefore, of practical moment.

Urban Development

This is an aspect of community welfare which has assumed considerable and increasing importance in South Pacific territories, but on which there is only meagre literature available. Town centres have grown up especially at the main ports of call for ocean vessels, and generally have ethnically complex populations.

The main urban centres in the central and eastern Pacific, Suva, Noumea, Papeete, and Apia, are now of considerable size. Together with the smaller settlements such as Levuka, Pago Pago, Nukualofa, and Avarua, they serve as magnets, drawing in from the outer areas for permanent or temporary residence the ambitious, the adventurous, the discontented and the curious, as well as many concerned with official, mission, and other business. Buses and taxis are busy plying the road systems, and the inter-island boats come and go.

Where even two decades ago the urban populations had proportionately few islanders as compared to Europeans, part-islanders, and Asiatics, their subsequent movement to the towns has been most marked. Problems of housing and sanitation, and even of unemployment, destitution, and delinquency, come increasingly to the forefront. Furthermore, Suva, and to a lesser extent Apia and the other communities mentioned, draw an increasing number of people from the small outer Territories, for which they form the hubs. These immigrants may sometimes now be living in miniature "colonies" in and around the town area. Suva, for example, has quite numerous Rotumans, Samoans, and Tongans, also some Gilbertese, Ellice islanders, and other island peoples. Papeete draws islanders from all outer zones of the French Establishments. As tendencies toward population growth combined with economic and educational stimulation operate in these outer island areas, further movements to such centres may confidently be expected.

The study of urban communities and of their constituent ethnic elements is not new to social anthropology, as witness a number of standard works since the well known "Middletown" survey of the 1920's. As regards this area, however, only passing references exist: see especially 80, 105, 155, 205, 288, 438, and 671. For any such community in the South Pacific, a comprehensive investigation would need to include demographic and ecological data on population groups; analyses of such matters as housing, employment, income, nutrition, social habits, and schooling; and investigation of the extent of active ties with home groups. The possibilities and problems of future expansion in urban populations could also be surveyed with profit. Paralleling the anthropological aspects of such studies, it might be considered useful to survey such economic facets as transportation, commercial and industrial development, and the entrepreneur role of the centre concerned in relation to its satellite communities and with the outer world.

Displaced Populations: Disaster Conditions

A feature of Pacific island history has been the displacement of populations, sometimes under emergency conditions, with consequent need for resettlement. Among the causes have been hurricanes, seismic ("tidal") waves, volcanic action, failures of food supply, pressures arising from over-population, missionary impetus toward community concentration, public works needs, commercial development, military requirements for restricted areas, and actual war operations such as those of the recent Pacific campaigns. The experiences which the governments and peoples concerned have had in making such adjustments appear highly pertinent in relation to any future resettlement needs.

The importance of this topic of population displacement in the thinking of anthropologists is indicated by the fact that the Society for Applied Anthropology (U.S.), at its 1950 annual meeting made it the subject of a special symposium. The main presentation dealt with the experience of the Bikini people who, following use of their island for atomic experimentation, have been resettled successively at several different places in the Marshall Islands (943). Very little detailed information is available, however, in the anthropological or other literature to date on such population shifts in the Pacific island areas, though there are a number of brief references, e.g., for the Gilberts (558); for Manihiki and Rakahanga (615); for Saipan and Guam (949), and for Mokil in the Carolines (945). The dislocations and devastation in Micronesian islands prior to the Japanese expulsion and in the early stages of United States military occupation are reviewed by Oliver (946). Relevant homesteading experiments for the resettlement of landless Hawaiians have been reported on by Keesing (940).

Among the significant cases which come to mind for consideration for more detailed study are the following: transfer of two groups of Samoans in Western Samoa from Savai'i island to Upolu because of a volcanic eruption, and their establishment in new villages there (1905); the projected return of some of these Samoan people to their home area on Savai'i in the near future; resettlement of Gilbertese from overcrowded areas in the Gilberts to the Phoenix Islands; resettlement of Banabans (Ocean Islanders) on Rambi island in Fiji after the war, because of phosphate-mining operations on their home island; the removal of the Nauruans to the Carolines by the Japanese during the war; removal of the population of Niuafo'ou island in the Tonga group, because of volcanic eruptions, and the effects of occasional devastating storms and seismic waves upon a number of islands. Anthropologists are particularly capable of making the intensive studies required to record such experiences of population displacement.

Disaster conditions such as destructive storms, high waves, volcanic outbreaks, and failures in food supply may not involve actual displacements of population but may call, nevertheless, for precautionary and rehabilitation measures. Some governments have established emergency regulations to meet hurricane warnings. The effectiveness of such measures, particularly in relation to the indigenous communities, might valuably be assessed. The availability of relief measures in case of disaster, such as Red Cross aid, though not the concern of the anthropologist except as he might examine their operation within such communities, is of regional concern. Longer term rehabilitation measures which have been tried by governments and local communities could also be studied profitably for their general significance. This topic probably deserves higher priority than the study of actual population displacements.

Emigration

Islanders and part-islanders have moved not only into other Territories within the South Pacific area, but also abroad to the metropolitan countries or elsewhere. Already small "colonies" are located here and there overseas, particularly Samoans in New Zealand, Sydney, Hawaii, and the United States mainland, and Cook islanders, Niueans, Tokelauans and others in New Zealand. Trainees from various Territories are also outside the area in colleges and other institutions. Anthropologists would not be concerned with the often difficult immigration laws and other attendant administrative questions involved. But they might be helpful in the future in investigating and so contributing to an understanding of these overseas groups.

The most urgent needs in this connexion appear to be related to the adjustment of such groups in the city of Auckland, New Zealand. Besides drawing in some 11,000 Maoris, or one out of every ten of this indigenous Polynesian group, this urban centre has most of the 2,000 Cook islanders, the 900 Samoans, and smaller numbers of other islanders, now in that Dominion. The problems of housing, employment, some inevitable degree of discrimination, and social welfare generally, have become quite serious, and government welfare services are being kept busy. Undoubtedly increasing numbers of islanders will want to try themselves out here and in other outside urban centres as population pressures and the rising level of ambitions make the island world more restrictive.

E

IV

HEALTH

AT FIRST sight it might not be thought that anthropologists could contribute significantly in the field of health and medical problems. Yet considerable attention has been given in anthropological writings to the general context of disease conditions and of birth and death, also to indigenous medical practices and practitioners, nutrition, child rearing including infant feeding, and their attendant ideologies, religious and otherwise. This material, however, much more than with most other subjects, is scattered widely in the literature. A general summary is essayed by Keesing (105, chapter X).

Disease Conditions and Treatment

Anthropologists have made only passing references to the incidence of diseases old and new in this area, including mental disorders. But they have usually listed the local nomenclature for such diseases, and given some exposition of the methods of diagnosis and the general ideas and beliefs surrounding them.

Many anthropological writers have pointed out that to the islanders, health, disease, and death were, and still largely are, saturated with supernaturalism. Modern approaches in medical work, therefore, usually have to compete with conservative magical and other practices, and with the entrenched influence of their traditional practitioners. Here, particularly, the anthropologist is the only expert who can provide extensive background information. But much more needs to be done in this field, particularly in collaboration with medical men working on specific problems.

The works most specifically focused on diseases, their mental settings, and their treatments are studies by Rougier and Spencer on the Fijians (283, 289), Collocott for Tonga (336); Hogbin for Ongtong Java (913); and Handy and Livermore for Hawaii (938). Other main references are as follows: 30, 32, 44, 64, 87, 89, 91, 105, 115, 116, 117, 151, 155, 163 (general); 221, 240, 245, 252, 263, 266a, 274, 277, 284, 295, 296, 309, 310, 318 (Fiji); 322, 323, 341, 367 (Tonga); 388, 427, 438, 441, 444, 476, 485, 490, 491, 502, 503a, 507, 509 (Samoa); 520

(Tokelaus); 534, 536, 546, 552, 558, 564 (Gilberts and Ellices); 581, 591 (Nauru); 595, 596 (Wallis and Horne); 603, 604, 614, 615, 616, 620, 623, 624, 625, 634, 636, 637, 639 (Cooks); 659, 660 (Niue); 673, 681, 708, 716 (Societies); 774, 785, 788, 789, 796, 805 (Tuamotus); 811, 817, 821, 826 (Gambiers); 828 (Australs); 852, 853, 855, 860, 871, 892, 893 (Marquesas); 906, 907, 909, 911, 919, 922, 924, 925 (Polynesian outliers).

Anthropological accounts sometimes include quite extensive discussions of disease treatments, such as massage and other types of physical manipulation; crude surgery; herbal and other remedies in which some of the local pharmacopoeias appear quite rich, and for most types of morbidity the inevitable ritual and other practices which, students have often pointed out, give the patient a psycho-somatic "lift" as being the equivalent of the "bedside manner" and other accompaniments of a modern medical treatment. Occasionally actual observed cases are described in these accounts; see, for example, in 277, 289, 295, 318, 336, 441, 659, 789.

Doctors generally discount such local medical lore, and some administrations have tried with indifferent success to forbid its practice. But a few medical men have interested themselves in the possible usefulness of some indigenous practices as being capable of supplementing Western-style treatments or of bridging the way to their acceptance. Some anthropologists have made a case for the importance of magical and other ritual aids as bolstering the sense of psychological welfare until such time as modern medical practices arouse the same confident faith. Whatever the viewpoints of medical administrators on these matters, they are likely to want more information regarding this context of indigenous medical practice. It is a field in which additional research is needed, though perhaps best done by private institutions and scholars except as it may bear directly upon specific projects formulated by the Commission, e.g., as relating to such diseases as tuberculosis or filariasis being actually studied. Collaboration is needed here with medical men, and also with botanists and others where necessary to identify local medical remedies.

Preventive Medicine: Sanitation

It is a commonplace in the island areas that customary conditions and usages must be taken into account in dealing with these problems.

Efforts to improve housing conditions (see "Housing" p. 42), water supplies, garbage disposal, latrines, quarantine against infectious diseases, mosquito and fly control, and various other health measures have frequently run foul of local "indifference" or even opposition. Anthropologists have some recorded materials here, as on water supply, disposal of human waste and of rubbish, and the general context of health measures, and they have collaborated to a minor extent with medical authorities on the problems involved. But the work done falls far short of the potential usefulness of their techniques of approach. A considerably greater amount has been done in this field in American Micronesia, particularly in analysing the general community and household settings in which preventive measures must operate.

Old Age: Death and Handling of the Dead

The death rate factor has been discussed earlier under "Population" (p. 12). Anthropologists turn up much material relating to the status of old people, and also to death and disposal of the dead, the latter obviously one of the major crises for individual and community (referred to in many of the works listed above, particularly the following: 30, 64, 89, 213, 221, 240, 245, 266a, 277, 289, 295, 296, 323, 336, 441, 457, 536, 632, 637, 659, 788, 817, 821, 855, 871, 919). In most of the island societies old age is respected, and elders still have useful functions and few problems of security. But there is now an increasing tendency to by-pass elders, as in our own society. Every comprehensive ethnological survey has a section on the handling of the dead, and on concepts relating to death, but usually dealing most fully with past practices and beliefs which may or may not persist. For the medical worker, adequate anthropological data of this kind may have varied uses, as for example where sanitation is affected by the presence of cemeteries, or where people are afraid to die in hospitals because of spirit beliefs, and are thus reluctant to enter them.

Adult and Infant Nutrition

This topic has been considered for convenience with "Food Habits" (chapter II, p. 22).

Infant and Maternal Welfare

From the anthropological viewpoint, this is largely bound up with the local forms of social organization, particularly family and household settings, as discussed under "Social Systems," (p. 43) and also child rearing practices, discussed under "Food Habits; Nutrition" and "Education" (pp. 22, 36). As part of any Commission projects on these aspects of welfare, it is highly recommended that anthropological expertness be enlisted in the work team or teams involved. The topic of birth is made a section of any standard anthropological monograph, and usually includes reference to customary practices and ideas relating to pregnancy, delivery methods, including use of special practitioners if any, ritual observances, early care of the infant, and later weaning practices. The most important references are 116, 138, 248, 252, 263, 277, 289, 295, 313, 323, 341, 441, 454, 457, 476, 503, 564, 591, 605, 620, 630, 635, 636, 637, 639, 721, 789, 871, 883, 912, 913.

Medical Personnel

Passing references are made in the anthropological literature to the work of trained island medical practitioners, nurses and other technical personnel, and also of women's health committees in local communities. Their activities come to the notice of anthropological field workers, for example, as being an excellent way of "indigenizing" what would otherwise remain a foreign system of medical work. But no systematic attempt has been made to evaluate their activities and problems in the intimate community settings. This matter might deservedly be studied more directly, in part through the anthropological approach, by the Commission or otherwise. Furthermore, it could well receive high priority, not least of all because of its importance in relation to the larger question of developing competent local leadership. A number of citations to useful research and writing done by such medical practitioners are included in the bibliography (142, 309, 310, 313, 341, 444, 454, 503, 536, 547).

V

RESEARCH NEEDS AND POSSIBILITIES

THE FOLLOWING is a summary of the various suggestions made under the previous topical headings, distinguished into the following categories:

I. Projects for possible incorporation into the regular Commission work programme or any technical assistance programme, with high priority, and capable of being handled by anthropological specialists working mainly alone, though consulting as necessary with any other technical specialists.

II. Projects in the same category, but suited more to anthropologists working as members of a team with other technical specialists.

III. Projects which the Commission might undertake in due course, but not having the same high priority.

IV. Projects best suited to research work by private institutions and scholars or under the auspices of local Governments, though usually involving significant information which the Commission could utilize as background to its more sharply focused problems, having regional significance.

V. Matters on which anthropologists might be called upon for minor consultation and advice.

(Note might be taken here once more of the remarks relating to personnel made at the end of chapter I.)

I. *Commission programme; high priority; anthropological specialists mainly working alone.*

1. The current status of agriculture, both for subsistence and for commerce, in selected indigenous communities, in relation to possible improvement and diversification, and to wider dissemination of useful local technical experience (p. 14). This should deal both with traditional crops such as the coconut and

with any introduced crops such as coffee and cocoa. One phase of such study should be concerned with the position on low islands (p. 31). In addition to the technical aspects of production, distribution, and consumption, emphasis should be laid on the wider economic and social context of agriculture. This project could be incorporated with II, 2, below.

2. Similar studies of the most important marine products, particularly as relating to shore fisheries and subsistence uses (p. 17); could be incorporated with II, 3.

3. Food handling and consumption in its economic and social context in selected communities, including both locally produced and imported foods; infant, child, and adult diets (p. 22); could be incorporated with II, 5-8.

4. A region-wide survey of indigenous methods of preserving and storing foods, as a basis for evaluation, possible improvement, and wider dissemination (p. 24); could be incorporated with II, 8.

5. The current hand-craft situation among groups where commercial marketing of hand-crafts seems feasible (p. 20); could be incorporated with II, 4.

6. The economic and social contexts of modern commercial development in selected communities: trading, organization of work, leadership, use of money, saving, banking and credit, etc. (pp. 25, 26, 30, 43).

7. The role and contribution, in given Territories or significant zones of Territories, of individuals from among the local peoples who have acquired, through educational institutions or otherwise, various types of vocational or technical training, as in administrative, commercial, medical, teaching, and other fields, as a basis for evaluating present and future personnel needs and problems (p. 39, d).

8. Community centres and their improvement, studied in the wider contexts of current community conditions and regional social customs (pp. 40, 43).

9. Childbirth and motherhood practices, and care of young children, in selected groups as background to infant and maternal welfare work (p. 24); see also II, 6.

II. *Commission programme; high priority; anthropologists working with other technical specialists.*

1. Population trends in crucial island settings, especially as relating to potential over-population. This should include attention to low and small islands (pp. 12, 31).

2. Anthropological participation in any specific agricultural project undertaken by the Commission, e.g., coconut improvement (p. 14); see also I, 1; III, 1.

3. Anthropological participation in any specific fisheries project (p. 17); see also I, 2; III, 2-5.

4. Organization of hand-craft industry where market outlets are available (p. 20); see also I, 5.

5. The problem of quantitative analysis of food consumption, including everyday and ceremonial foods (p. 22).

6. Evaluation of infant diets in terms of their nutritional value, also maternal diets and weaning customs (p. 24); see also I, 3.

7. Evaluation of other diets, including those of young children, school-children, adults, and labouring groups (p. 22); see also I, 3.

8. Improvement of methods of preserving and storing food (p. 24); see also I, 4.

9. Needs for capital and credit in selected indigenous groups (p. 26); see also I, 6.

10. Possibly certain aspects of sea transport problems (p. 27); see V, 1.

11. Property tenure problems as specifically arising from any Commission project (p. 28).

12. Study of work habits as part of anthropological participation in any Commission development project (p. 30).

13. Preparation of school curricula, texts, and supplementary teaching materials in relation to regional conditions, to indigenous ideas and activities, and to English or French language competence (p. 38, c).

14. Vocational and other needs and outlets for advanced schooling (p. 39, d); see also I, 7.

15. The social context of mass literacy and adult education generally (p. 40, f).

16. Detailed anthropological survey of any community selected for a community development project (p. 40).

17. The existing housing situation in any group selected for experimental housing improvement (p. 42).

18. The economic and social background of co-operative society schemes (p. 28).

19. The indigenous contexts of particular diseases being studied in the Commission programme, e.g., filariasis, tuberculosis, taking groups in which they have particular importance, and taking account of local ideologies and methods of treatment (p. 56).

III. *Commission long-term programme; lower priority.*

1. Preparation of materials on agricultural methods (exhibits, slides, diagrams, text materials) from both inside and outside the area with a view to disseminating ideas which might bring about improvement (p. 14).

2. The same for fishing methods (p. 17).

3. Indigenous techniques of open sea fishing (p. 17).

4. Anthropological data relevant to the problem of introducing pond fisheries (p. 18).

5. The use of marine plant life for foods and other purposes (p. 17).

6. The indigenous contexts relating to livestock improvement (p. 19).

7. The best raw materials suited to hand-craft production, their present availability, and wider dissemination (p. 21).

8. Forestry knowledge and utilization of products among selected groups, as specifically relevant to forestry programmes (p. 22).

9. The problems associated with converting indigenous land rights into modern type legal titles (p. 28).

10. Indigenous work habits in selected groups, examined in terms of their productivity; possible opportunities and also hazards relating to mechanization; this could possibly go under I.

11. Differential school training for boys and girls (pp. 38, c; 39, d).

12. Home science training, especially for girls and women (pp. 38, c; 39, d).

13. Bilingualism as an objective of schooling (p. 39, e).

14. Preparation of materials for, and evaluation of experiments with, audio-visual aids, including broadcasting (p. 40, f).

15. Preparation of materials on housing (exhibits, slides, diagrams, text materials) from both inside and outside the area with a view to disseminating ideas which might bring about improvement (p. 42).

16. The indigenous contexts of sanitation and other measures of preventive medicine: garbage disposal, latrines, etc.; formulation of practical plans to meet needs and minimize conflict (p. 57).

17. The indigenous medical worker in his community setting (p. 59).

IV. *Private institutions or scholars; local Governments sponsoring where appropriate.*

1. General delineation of existing economic systems, with emphasis on contemporary trends (p. 8).

2. Adjustment of peoples to various types of island habitats (p. 8).

3. Population trends and their analysis (p. 12).

4. Fertility (birth rates) in the island societies, with particular attention to the problems involved in lowering high birth rates (p. 12).

5-8. The present status of agriculture among the various population elements, with emphasis on contemporary trends (p. 14). Similar basic studies of marine products (p. 17), livestock (p. 19), and hand-crafts (p. 20).

9. Forests in relation to indigenous economies, including basic knowledge, property rights, and utilization of products (p. 22).

10. Foods and their preparation today (p. 22).

11. Nutritional problems as listed under I, II, (p. 22).

12. Commercial concepts and practices in the indigenous economic and social settings of today, including the role of the trading store (p. 25).

13. Present status of traditional exchange practices, ceremonial wealth, and associated customs (p. 25).

14. Studies of surpluses and savings, and associated ideas and habits (p. 26).

15. The place of money in present-day island economies (p. 26).

16. The position of the more "enterprising" islanders who come strongly under the influence of the money economy, if possible with case histories (p. 26).

17. Changes brought about by the development of modern transport and communication; continuing place of traditional sea and land transport (p. 27).

18. Indigenous property customs today, especially relating to land tenure and marine rights, and including modifications brought about by commercial concepts, e.g., land transactions; landlordism (p. 28).

19. Customs of inheritance today (p. 28).

20. Work habits in their wider economic and social context (p. 30).

21. Changes in work habits induced by the needs of modern population growth and accessibility to urban centres (p. 30).

22. Work obligations and related demands upon the time of the individual for community maintenance (p. 30).

23. Labour union organization and its impact upon island societies where it has penetrated (p. 30).

24. Economic and social adaptations involved in living on the various types of low and small islands, with emphasis on present-day conditions (p. 31).

25. Emigration from the low islands and establishment of "colonics" elsewhere (p. 31).

26. Factors favouring and militating against the development of independent smallholding among indigenous groups (p. 34).

27. The smallholder system in Tonga, as yielding data significant for the problems of other areas (p. 34).

28. The development of smallholding in Fiji by Fijians, Indians and others (p. 34).

29. The status and problems of part-islanders engaged in agricultural pursuits (p. 35).

30. Child training today in selected groups (p. 38, b).

31. Personality development and personality (character structure) in general in selected groups (pp. 38, b; 46).

32. The role of the elementary school and schoolteacher in selected communities (p. 38, c).

33. The needs for more advanced schooling and for vocational training in selected areas; the activities of individuals with such more advanced education to date (p. 39, d).

34. Education of non-indigenous population groups (p. 40, g).

35. Patterns of settlement today in significant areas (p. 40).

36. Detailed studies of representative single communities (p. 40).

37. Housing in its total economic and social context (p. 42).

38. Continued delineation of existing social systems, with emphasis on analysis of acculturation processes (p. 43).

39. Detailed life histories of individuals (p. 44).

40. Religion and mission work in contemporary societies (p. 46).

41. "Nativistic" or "adjustment" movements (p. 46).

42. Continuing delineation of basic ideologies and value systems inherent in the island cultures, and of clashes and adjustments with Western-style values (p. 47).

43. Art and leisure activities today, and their important social functions (p. 48).

44. Co-operative and individualistic activities in the indigenous communities, including the loci of elective behaviour and authoritarian conformity (p. 50).

45. Social disorganization and delinquency in various community settings (p. 51).

46. Urban community studies, including the place of the various ethnic groups; ecology, economics, social organization, political role, leisure activities, education, etc. (p. 52).

47. The position of emigrant islanders abroad (p. 55).

48. The nature and incidence of mental diseases in selected groups (p. 56).

49. The present-day practice of indigenous style medicine (p. 56).

50. The context of death and handling of the dead (p. 58).

51. Old age in the indigenous societies (p. 58).

52. Birth and early care of children (p. 24); see also 30 above.

53. The work of medical practitioners, nurses, and other trained health personnel in indigenous settings (p. 59).

V. *Anthropological consultation and advice (some examples only).*

1. Sea and land transport problems, though this item might possibly be transferred to II for certain aspects (p. 27).
2. Water supply problems on low islands (p. 31).
3. The experimental introduction of any new technical feature as part of a "technical assistance" programme, e.g., refrigeration, power, mechanization.
4. Preparation of literature for village libraries (p. 36 ff).
5. Expansion of inter-island contacts and stimulation of regionally valuable pursuits, as through festivals, sports, exhibits, and other activities (p. 48).
6. Tourist trade stimulation, in respect of entertainment programmes, travel, protection, etc. (p. 48).
7. Conservation of archaeological and historical sites and objects (p. 48).
8. Sanitation measures of specific character, such as latrine types, mosquito and fly control, including proposals for low island welfare (p. 57).
9. Training of island medical personnel (p. 59).

The above topical list does not attempt to suggest specific Territories or localities in which any particular project might be carried out. The choice of locale for a project is not only a matter of an existing need for research, but also of the personal background and interest of the particular scholar who might be available, his language competence, and other unpredictable factors. As will be seen by anyone who examines carefully the survey of what has been done in social anthropology to date, every Territory can profit by further research work, especially on current conditions. Any worker coming into the field will find no difficulty in by-passing the problems and localities which have been or are being effectively covered so as to be able to break new ground in any of the Territories concerned.

SELECT BIBLIOGRAPHY

THIS bibliography contains all important titles so far uncovered by the writer which are relevant to the problems of social anthropology. It does not include references to the "physical anthropology," "archaeology," and "linguistics" of the area unless these have materials relevant to the above: a bibliography of linguistic materials would be a particularly long one in itself.

In addition to the writings of professionally-recognized anthropologists, such a bibliography must also contain many works by other observers dealing with anthropological subjects, including government officials, missionaries, natural scientists, journalists, and indeed scholars calling themselves "anthropologists" in days before the more rigorous standards and techniques of the present-day science were developed. Many of these works are of great value, especially as source materials for more technical scholarship. The selection of titles here, however, has necessarily to be somewhat arbitrary. The writer has chosen the following principles to guide such selection:

(1) No work previous to about 1890, when anthropological field work of reasonably modern calibre was getting under way, is included unless it has materials of outstanding importance.

(2) No official documents (government reports, laws, etc.), missionary materials (reports to mission bodies, references in mission magazines, etc.), ships' logs (as with the voyages of exploration), or travellers' narratives are included unless they have reasonably extensive materials of ethnological importance.

(3) Recent writings by local residents, journalists, and others are included only if they supply important source materials which a professional scholar may find useful (this type of reference occurs most frequently in the lists for eastern Polynesian groups, on which up-to-date technical studies are fewer).

A more general bibliography prepared by C. R. H. Taylor, Librarian of the Turnbull Library, Wellington, published by the Polynesian Society, contains many early and more marginal references omitted here. It also supplies references for Polynesian groups and areas not included as falling outside the scope of the South Pacific Commission:

the Hawaiians, Maoris of New Zealand, and Easter and Pitcairn islands.

The writer would be glad if omissions noted by readers—and such omissions are especially likely to occur as regards source materials in French and German—could be sent to the Executive Officer for Social Development, South Pacific Commission, as the basis for a supplementary list.

A system of asterisks has been adopted to give a general sense of the importance of each work in relation to the Commission's interest in social anthropology, as well as the professional competence of the work involved. Two asterisks (**) indicate a reference of major significance, both professionally and from the viewpoint of modern "applied" problems. One asterisk (*) indicates a reference of some importance, e.g., a professionally accepted work on some minute or technical theme without much "applied" significance, or a fairly professional job on some important theme. Absence of an asterisk indicates a reference which, though it may be worth-while in its own right, is marginal to social anthropology, yet may be a useful source for materials.

It will be noticed that in many citations the date is followed by the letters a, b, etc. This is used where one author has written more than one work in the same year, to establish the order in which they were written.

Serials

The following are the main journals and bulletins in which materials appear. With them are given any abbreviations by which they will receive reference in the sections which follow.

American Anthropologist (A.A.)
Anthropos (An.)
Australasian Association for the Advancement of Science Reports
  (A.A.A.S.R.)
Australian Geographer (A.G.)
B.P. Bishop Museum, Bulletins (B.M.B.)
B.P. Bishop Museum, Memoirs (B.M.M.)
B.P. Bishop Museum, Occasional Papers (B.M.O.P.)
B.P. Bishop Museum, Special Publications (B.M.S.P.)
Geographical Journal (G.J.)
Geographical Review (G.R.)

l'Anthropologie (l'Anth.)
Man (Man)
New Zealand Geographer (N.Z.G.)
Oceania (Oc.)
Pacific Science Congress, Proceedings (P.S.C.P.)
Polynesian Society, Journal (P.S.J.)
Polynesian Society, Memoirs (P.S.M.)
Royal Anthropological Institute, Journal (R.A.I.J.)
Société des Etudes Océaniennes, Bulletins (S.E.O.B.)
Société des Océanistes, Journal (S.O.J.)
Zeitschrift für Ethnologie (Z.E.)

The entries are grouped under the following headings:—

General

ALEXANDER, A. B.
  1** Notes on the boats, apparatus and fishing methods employed by the natives of the south sea islands, in *U.S. Fish Commission, Report,* 743-829. 1901.

ALEXANDER, W. D.
  2 Ancient systems of land tenure in Polynesia, *Friend,* April, 26-27; May, 36-37; June, 47-49. 1888.

ANDERSEN, J. C.
  3* *Myths and legends of the Polynesians.* London. 1928.
  4* *Maori music with its Polynesian background.* P.S.M. 10. 1934.

ARCHEY, G.
  5** *South Sea folk.* Auckland Museum, Handbook for Oceanic Ethnology (2nd edition). 1949.

AUCKLAND INSTITUTE AND MUSEUM
  6 *Food is where you find it; a guide to emergency foods of the western Pacific.* Auckland. 1943.

BASTIAN, A.
  7 *Inselgruppen in Ozeanien.* Berlin. 1883.
  8 *Einiges aus Samoa und andern Inseln der Südsee* . . . Berlin. 1889.

BATESON, G.
  9** Arts of the South Seas, *The Art Bulletin*, 28, 119-23. New York. 1946.

BEAGLEHOLE, E.
  10** Cultural peaks in Polynesia, *Man*, 37, No. 176. 1937a.
  11** Polynesian anthropology today, *A.A.*, 39, 213-21. 1937b.
  12** Government and administration in Polynesia, in *Specialized studies in Polynesian anthropology.* B.M.B. 193. 1947.

BEAGLEHOLE, J. C.
  13 *The exploration of the Pacific.* London. 1934.

BEASLEY, H. G.
  14* Some Polynesian cuttlefish baits, *R.A.I.J.*, 51, 100-14. 1921.
  15* *Pacific island records: fishhooks.* London. 1928.

BECKWITH, M. W.
  16* *Hawaiian mythology.* New Haven. (Includes comparative materials from other Polynesian areas.) 1940.

BELL, F. L. S.
  17** The place of food in the social life of central Polynesia, *Oceania*, 2, 117-35. 1931.
  18** A functional interpretation of inheritance and succession in central Polynesia, *Oceania*, 3, 167-206. 1932.

BEST, E.
  19 *Polynesian voyagers.* Dominion Museum Memoir 5. 1923.
  20 *The Maori canoe . . . with some description of those of the isles of the Pacific.* Dominion Museum Bulletin 7, Wellington. 1925.

BRIGHAM, W. T.
  21 *An index to the islands of the Pacific Ocean.* B.M.M., 1, no. 2. 1900.
  22 *The ancient Hawaiian house.* B.M.M., 2, 3. (Includes comparative materials from other Polynesian areas.) 1908.

BRITISH MUSEUM
  23 *Handbook to the ethnological collections.* London. 1910.

F

BROWN, C.
24   Catalogue of the Crosby Brown collection of musical instruments . . . Instruments of the savage tribes . . . Part 2, Oceania. Metropolitan Museum of Art, Handbook 13. 1907.

BROWN, G.
25   Melanesians and Polynesians. London. 1910.

BROWN, J. M.
26   Peoples and problems of the Pacific. 2 vols. London. 1927.

BRYAN, E. H., Jr.
27   American Polynesia and the Hawaiian chain. Honolulu. 1942.

BUCK, P. H. (Te Rangi Hiroa)
28** Polynesian education . . . , The Friend (Honolulu), 1928, 227-28; 1931, 56-58. 1928, 1931.
29*   Polynesian oratory, in E.S.C. Handy and others, Ancient Hawaiian civilization. Honolulu. 161-68. 1932.
30** Regional diversity in the elaboration of sorcery in Polynesia. Yale University Publications in Anthropology, 2. 1936.
31** Vikings of the sunrise. New York. 1938.
32** Anthropology and religion. New Haven. 1939.
33*   The study of Polynesian material culture, Mankind, 3, 1-6. 1941.
34** The disappearance of canoes in Polynesia, P.S.J., 51, 191-99. 1942.
35** Arts and crafts of the Cook Islands. B.M.B. 179, 473-526 (Historical reconstruction of culture processes in Polynesia). 1944.
36** An introduction to Polynesian anthropology. B.M.B. 187 (with comprehensive bibliographies). 1945.
37*   The coming of the Maori. Wellington. 1949.

BURROWS, E. G.
38*   Polynesian part-singing, Zeitschrift für Vergleichende Musikwissenschaft, 2, 69-88. 1934.
39*   Western Polynesia, a study in cultural differentiation. Etnologiska Studier, 7, 1-192. 1938.
40** Breed and border in Polynesia, A.A., 41, 1-21. 1939.
41** Polynesian music and dancing, P.S.J., 49, 331-346. 1940a.
42** Culture areas in Polynesia, Idem, 49, 349-63. 1940b.
43** Functional and psychological studies in Polynesia in Specialized studies in Polynesian anthropology. B.M.B. 193, 75-85. 1947.

BUXTON, P. A.
44*   Researches in Polynesia and Melanesia. London School of Hygiene and Tropical Medicine, Memoir 2, parts 5-7. 1928.

CAILLOT, A. C. E.
45*   Les Polynésiens orientaux au contact de la civilisation. Paris. 1909.
46*   Histoire de la Polynésie oriental. Paris. 1910.
47*   Mythes, légendes et traditions des Polynésiens. Paris. 1914.

CARR, D.
48*   A note on Polynesian orthography, P.S.J., 49, 564-68. 1940.

CHRISTIAN, F. W.
49* On the distribution and origin of some plant and tree names in Polynesia and Micronesia, *P.S.J.*, 6, 123-40. 1897.
50* *Eastern Pacific lands.* London. 1910.

CHURCHILL, W.
51 *The Polynesian wanderings.* Carnegie Institution of Washington, Publication 134. 1911.
52 *Club types of nuclear Polynesia. Idem*, Publication 255. 1917.

COULTER, J. W.
53 Environment, race and government in south sea islands, *Scottish Geographical Magazine*, 63, 49-56. 1947.

DAMM, H.
54* *Die gymnastischen Spiele der Indonesier und Südseevölker.* 1. Teil: *Die Zweikampfspiele.* Staatliche Forschungsinstitut in Leipzig, Institut für Völkerkunde. Leipzig. 1922.
55* Das Tika-spiel der Polynesier, *Baessler-Archiv. Beiträge zur Völkerkunde*, 19, 1-2, 5-15. 1936.

DAVIDSON, D. S.
56 The Pacific and circum-Pacific appearances of the dart-game, *P.S.J.*, 45, 99-114; 46, 1-23. 1936-7.
57 The antiquity of man in the Pacific and the question of trans-Pacific migrations, in McCurdy, G. G. (editor), *Early Man.* Philadelphia. 1937.
58* *Oceania. The Oceanic collections of the University Museum.* University of Pennsylvania, Museum Bulletin 12, nos. 3-4. Philadelphia. 1947.

DENSMORE, F.
59 *Handbook of the collection of musical instruments in the United States National Museum.* Smithsonian Institution, U.S. National Museum Bulletin 136. Washington. 1927.

DESCAMPS, P.
60* Le rôle social de la pirogue, *l'Anth.* 33, 127-45. 1923.

DIXON, R. B.
61 *The mythology of all races*, Vol. 9 (*Oceania*). Boston. 1916.
62 The problem of the sweet potato in Polynesia, *A.A.*, 34, 1, 40-46. 1932.

DODGE, E. S.
63* *Gourd growers of the south seas.* Salem. 1943.

DOERR, E.
64* Bestattungsformen in Ozeanien, *An.* 30, 369-420, 727-65. 1935.

DORSENNE, J.
65 *Polynésie.* Paris. 1929.

DOUGLAS, A. J. A.
66 *The south seas of today.* London. 1926.

DUNBABIN, T.
67 *Slavers of the south seas.* Sydney. 1935.

ECKERT, G.
68* Der Einfluss der Familien-organisation auf die Bevölkerungs-
bewegung in Ozeanien, *An.* 31, 789-99. 1936.

EDGE-PARTINGTON, J. and HEAPE, C.
69* *Ethnological album of the Pacific islands.* Series 1-3. Manchester. 1890-98.

ELLIS, W.
70   *Polynesian researches.* vols. 1-2. London. 1829.

EMORY, K. P.
71** *South sea lore.* B.M.S.P. 36. 1934.
72* Polynesian stone remains, *Studies in the anthropology of Oceania and Asia.*
Harvard Peabody Museum, Papers, 20. Cambridge. 1943.

FESTETICS DE TOLNA, R.
73   *Chez les cannibales. Huit ans de croisière dans l'Océan Pacifique à bord du
yacht "Le Tolna."* Paris. 1903.

FINSCH, O.
74   Ethnologische Erfahrung und Belegstücke aus der Südsee. Wien. 1893.

FIRTH, R.
75** Totemism in Polynesia, *Oc.*, 1, 291-321, 377-98. 1930-31.
76** The analysis of mana, *P.S.J.*, 49, 483-512. 1940.

FORNANDER, A.
77   *The Polynesian race.* vols. 1-3. London. 1878-85.

FRAZER, J. G.
78   *The belief in immortality and the worship of the dead. Vol. I:
The belief . . . (in) Melanesia. Vol. II: The belief among the Polynesians.
Vol. III:
The belief among the Micronesians.* London. 1913-24.

FRIEDERICI, G.
79* Das Auslegergeschirr der Südsee-boote, *Ethnologischer Anzeiger,* 3, 4,
187-201. 1933.

FURNAS, J. C.
80   *Anatomy of Paradise.* New York. 1946.

GILL, L. T.
81* Migrations of food plants in the Pacific, *Pan-Pacific Research Institution,
Journal,* April-June, 7-9. 1934.

GOULD, W. H.
82* Education of the Polynesian, in *The Maori and education,* edited bv
Jackson, P. M. Wellington. 1931.

GREINER, R. A.
83* *Polynesian decorative designs.* B.M.B. 7. 1923.

GUDGER, E. W.
84* Wooden hooks used for catching sharks and ruvettus in the south seas,
American Museum of Natural History, Anthropological Papers, 28, 212-343.
1927.
85* The distribution of ruvettus, the oilfish, throughout the south seas

as shown by the distribution of the peculiar wooden hook used in its capture, *American Naturalist*, 62, 467-77. 1928.

HAMBRUCH, P.

86* *Südseemärchen aus Australien, Neu Guinea, Fidji, Karolinen, Samoa, Tonga* ... Jena. 1921.

HAMY, E. T.

87 Les Polynésiens et leur extinction, *La Nature*, Paris, 1, 89, 13 February, 161. 1875.

HANDY, E. S. C.

88 Some conclusions and suggestions regarding the Polynesian problem, *A.A.*, 22, 226-36. 1920.

89 *Polynesian religion.* B.M.B. 34. 1927.

90 *The problem of Polynesian origins*, B.M.O.P., 9, 8. 1930.

91** Perspectives in Polynesian religion, *P.S.J.*, 49, 309-30. 1940.

92** Forebears and posterity in the Pacific isles, *The Improvement Era*, 53, 8, 616-18, 677-79. 1950.

HEYERDAHL, T.

93 *Kon-Tiki.* New York. 1950.

HOCART, A. M.

94* Chieftainship and the sister's son in the Pacific, *A.A.*, 17, 4, 631-46. 1915.

HOGBIN, H. I.

95** Polynesian ceremonial gift exchanges, *Oc.*, 3, 13-39. 1932-33.

96** *Law and order in Polynesia.* London. 1934.

97** Mana, *Oc.*, 6, 241-74. 1936.

HORNELL, J.

98** *String figures from Fiji and western Polynesia.* B.M.B.39. 1927.

99** *The canoes of Polynesia, Fiji, and Micronesia, vol. 1: Canoes of Oceania.* B.M.S.P. 27. 1936.

100* Outrigger devices: distribution and origin, *P.S.J.*, 52, 91-100. 1943.

101 Was there pre-Columbian contact between the peoples of Oceania and South America? *P.S.J.*, 54, 157-91. 1945.

HUNTER, D.

102 The beating and decorating of bark paper in Tonga, Fiji and Samoa, in his *Primitive papermaking*, 35-47. London. 1927.

KEESING, F. M.

103** Standards of living among native peoples of the Pacific, *Pacific Affairs*, 8,1. 1935.

104** *Education in Pacific countries.* Shanghai and Honolulu. 1937.

105** *The south seas in the modern world.* London and Stanford. 1941.

106** *Native peoples of the Pacific world.* New York. 1945a.

107** Applied anthropology in colonial administration, in *The science of man in the world crisis*, (ed. Linton, Ralph,) 373-98. New York. 1945b.

108** Extension work in Pacific islands, in *Farmers of the world*, by E. de S. Brunner and others. New York. 1945c.

109** Acculturation in Polynesia, in *Specialized studies in Polynesian anthropology*, B.M.B. 193, 32-46. 1947.
110** *Cultural dynamics and administration*, Seventh P.S.C.P., 1948. Auckland. 1950a.
111* *The Pacific island peoples in the postwar world* (Condon Lectures, Oregon). Eugene. 1950b.

KEESING, M. M.
112** Education in Polynesia, in *Specialized studies in Polynesian anthropology*, B.M.B. 193, 47-57. 1946.

KENNEDY, R.
113* *The islands and peoples of the south seas and their cultures.* Philadelphia. 1945.

KRIEGER, H. W.
114* *Island peoples of the western Pacific: Micronesia and Melanesia.* Smithsonian Institution War Background Studies 16. Washington. 1943.

LAMBERT, S. M.
115** The depopulation of Pacific races, B.M.S.P. 23. 1934.
116** Medical conditions in the south Pacific, *Medical Journal, Australia*, September. 1938.
117* *A Yankee doctor in paradise.* New York. 1941.

LARSEN, H.
118 Some ancient specimens from western and central Polynesia in *Ethnographical studies published on the occasion of the centenary of the Ethnographical Department, National Museum, Copenhagen*, 220-50. 1941.

LEENHARDT, M.
119** *Arts de l'Océanie*, Paris. 1951.

LEHMANN, F. R.
120* *Die polynesischen Tabusitten.* Leipzig. 1930.
121* *Die Adoption bei schriftlosen Völkern.* Tagungsbericht der Gesellschaft für Völkerkunde, 2. Leipzig. 1936

LESSON, P. A.
122 *Les Polynésiens.* Vols. 1-4. Paris. 1880-84.

LINTON, R.
123** *Ethnology of Polynesia and Micronesia.* Chicago (Field) Museum of Natural History, Guide Series, 6. 1926.

LINTON, R. and WINGERT, P. S.
124** *Arts of the south seas.* New York. 1946.

LOEB, E. M.
125* Die soziale Organization Indonesiens und Ozeaniens, An. 28, 649-62. 1933.
126* *The social organization of Oceania and the American northwest*, Sixth P.S.C.P., 1939, 4, 135-40. 1940.

LOVETT, R.
127 The history of the London Missionary Society, 1795–1895. Vols. 1–2. Oxford. 1899.
LUOMALA, K.
128* Documentary research in Polynesian mythology, P.S.J., 49, 175–95. 1940.
129** Missionary contributions to Polynesian anthropology, in Specialized studies in Polynesian anthropology, B.M.B. 193, 5–31. 1947.
130* Maui-of-a-thousand-tricks . . . B.M.B. 198. 1949.
131* The menehune of Polynesia and other mythical little people of Oceania. B.M.B. 203. 1951.
MACKENZIE, D. C.
132 Myths and traditions of the south sea islands. London. 1931.
MAGRE, H.
133 Le monde Polynésien. Paris. 1902.
MAKEMSON, M. W.
134* The morning star rises. New Haven. 1941.
MEAD, M.
135* An inquiry into the question of cultural stability in Polynesia. Columbia University Contributions to Anthropology, 9. 1928.
136** Education and cultural surrogates, Journal of Educational Sociology, 14, 2, 92–109. 1940.
137** The role of small south sea cultures in the post war world, A.A., 45, 193–96. 1943.
138** Research on primitive children, in Manual of child psychology, edited by Carmichael, L. New York. 1946.
MÜHLMANN, W. E.
139** Staatsbildung in Polynesien, Z.E., 65, 380–89. 1933.
140** Soziologische spekulation einer Adelkaste (South Seas), Forschungen und Fortschritte, 10, 16, 203–04. 1934.
141** Staatsbildung und Amphiktyonien in Polynesien: eine studie zur Ethnologie und politischen Soziologie. Stuttgart. 1938.
NATIVE MEDICAL PRACTITIONERS
142** Native Foodstuffs (Fiji, Ellice, etc.), Native Medical Practitioner, 3, 548–53 (26 recipes collected by practitioners.) 1941.
NGATA, A. T.
143** Anthropology and the government of native races, Australasian Journal of Psychology and Philosophy, 16, 1, 1–14. 1928.
OLDMAN, W. O.
144 Oldman collection of Polynesian artifacts. P.S.M., 15. 1938–40.
OLIVER, D. M.
145** The Pacific islands. New York. 1951.
O'REILLY, P.
146* Note sur les collections océaniennes des musées d'ethnographie de la Suisse, S.O.J., 2, 2, 109–27. 1946.

147* Bibliographie de l'Océanie, 1946, *S.O.J.*, 3,3, 173-202. (Useful compilation on a wide range of topics, continuing a series of bibliographic compilations in this journal by O'Reilly and Reitman, E.) 1947.

PALMER, G. B.
148* Mana. Some Christian and Moslem parallels. *P.S.J.*, 55, 263-76. 1947.

PAN-PACIFIC SCIENTIFIC CONFERENCE (FIRST)
149** *Recommendations for anthropological research in Polynesia*, Proceedings, 1920, 103-23. 1921.

PAULME, J. C. (EDITOR)
150* Océanie. *Légendes et récits Polynésiens extraits de son Bulletin et publiés par la Société d'Etudes Océaniennes de Papeete . . .*L'Exposition coloniale internationale. Paris. 1931.

PÉTARD, P.
151** Le ti. Cordyline terminalis. Ethno-botanique et médecine polynésienne. *S.O.J.*, 2, 194-208. 1946.

PHELPS, S.
152** *Puberty observances in Polynesia and Micronesia*, Sixth P.S.C.P. 4, 145-52. 1940.

PIDDINGTON, R.
153** *Methods of research in Polynesian ethnology*, Sixth P.S.C.P., 4, 81-84. 1940.

PITT-RIVERS, G.
154* *The clash of culture and the contact of races*. London. 1927.

PRICE, W. A.
155* *Nutrition and physical degeneration*. New York. 1939.

PRITCHARD, W. T.
156 *Polynesian reminiscences*. London. 1866.

QUATREFAGES, A. DE
157 *Les Polynésiens et leurs migrations*. Paris. 1866.

READ, C. H.
158* On the origin and sacred character of certain ornaments of the S.E. Pacific, *R.A.I.J.*, 21, 139-59. 1891.

REED, H. C.
159* How early Polynesians used the now neglected *pia* plant, *Pacific Islands Monthly*, 11, 8, 27-28. 1941.

RIESENBERG, F.
160 *The Pacific Ocean*. New York, London. 1940.

RIESENFELD, A.
161* *The megalithic culture of Melanesia*. Leiden. 1950.

RIVET, P.
162** *Les Océaniens*. Frazer lectures. London. 1932.

ROBERTS, S. H.
163 *Population problems of the Pacific*. London. 1927.

ROBSON, R. W. (EDITOR)
164   *The Pacific Islands Yearbook*, and *The Pacific Islands Monthly* (journal,
      containing frequent items of anthropological interest.) 1932-

SCHANZ, M.
165   *Australien und die Südsee*. Berlin. 1901.

SCHOLEFIELD, G. H.
166* *Economic revolution in Polynesia*, A.A.A.S.R., 16, 499-602. 1923.

SCHURTZ, H.
167   *Altersklassen und Männerbünde: eine Darstellung der Grundformen der
      Gesellschaft*. Berlin. 1902.

SKINNER, H. D.
168* Bowling discs from New Zealand and other parts of Polynesia, *P.S.J.*,
      55, 243-62. 1946.

SÖDERSTROM, J. A.
169** Some notes on poi and other preserved vegetables in the Pacific,
      Ethnos, 2, 235-42. 1937.
170* *A. Sparrman's ethnological collection from James Cook's 2nd expedition
      (1772-1775)*. Stockholm. 1939.

SPEISER, F.
171* Kulturgeschichtliche Betrachtungen über die Initiationen in der Südsee,
      Schweizerischen Gesellschaft für Anthropologie und Ethnologie, Bulletin,
      22, 28-61. Zurich. 1945-6.
172* Neu-Calédonien, die südlichen Neuen Hebriden und Polynesien.
      Verhändlungen der Naturforschenden Gesellschaft in Basel, 57. 1946a.
173* Versuch einer Siedlungsgeschichte der Südsee, *Denkschriften der Schwei-
      zerischen Naturforschenden Gesellschaft*, 77, 1, 1-81. Zurich. 1946b.

STANNER, W. E. H.
174   *The south seas in transition* (in preparation).

STOKES, J. F. G.
175   *The mat sails of the Pacific*, B.M.O.P., 1, 25-32. 1899.
176   Index to *The Polynesian race* by Abraham Fornander. B.M.S.P., 4. 1909.

SULLIVAN, L. R.
177* Race types in Polynesia, *A.A.*, 26, 22-26. 1924.

TISCHNER, H.
178** *Die Verbreitung der Hausformen in Ozeanien*. Studien zur Völkerkunde,
      7. Leipzig. 1934.
179* Les collections océaniennes d'ethnographie en Allemagne après la
      guerre, *S.O.J.*, 3, 3, 35-42. 1947.

TREAT, I.
180* South sea adventure in the kitchen, *The Geographical Magazine*, Febru-
      ary, 245-58. 1938.

WALKER, O.
181* *Tiurai le guérisseur*, S.E.O.B., 10, 1-35. 1925.

WECKLER, J. E.
182** *Polynesians, explorers of the Pacific.* Smithsonian Institution War Background Studies, 6. 1943.

WINGERT, P. S.
183* *Outline guide to the art of the South Pacific.* New York. 1946.

WILLIAMSON, R. W.
184   *The social and political systems of central Polynesia.* Vols. 1-3. Cambridge. 1924.
185   *Religious and cosmic beliefs of central Polynesia.* Vols. 1-2. Cambridge. 1933.
186   *Religion and social organization in Central Polynesia* (edited by Piddington, R.) Cambridge. 1937.
187   *Essays in Polynesian ethnology* (edited by Piddington, R.) Cambridge. 1939.

YUNCKER, T. G.
188*   Kava, its preparation and use, *Indiana Academy of Science, Proceedings,* 50, 60-71. 1941.

Fiji, including Lau and Rotuma

ADAMS, E. H.
189   *Jottings from the Pacific: life and incidents in the Fijian and Samoan islands.* London. 1890.

ALLARDYCE, W. L.
190   The Fijians in peace and war, *Man,* 45, 69-73. 1904a.
191   Fijians and their firewalking, *Royal Colonial Institute, Journal,* 35, 2, 105-11. 1904b.

ANDERSON, J. W.
192   *Notes of travel in Fiji and New Caledonia* . . . London. 1880.

BELTRAN Y ROZPIDE, R.
193   Islas Viti y Rotuma, *Sociedad Geografica de Madrid,* 12, 177-204. 1882.

BREWSTER, A. B.
194** *Hill tribes of Fiji.* Philadelphia and London. 1922.

BROMILOW, W. E.
195   *Twenty years among primitive Papuans* (Chapters 1, 2 deal with Fiji.) London. 1929.

BROWN, G.
196   Notebook and other papers (manuscripts). Mitchell Library, Sydney. 1897-.

BURTON, J. W.
197   *The Fiji of today.* London. 1910.

CAPELL, A. AND LESTER, R. H.
198** Local divisions and movements in Fiji, *Oc.,* 11, 4, 313-41; 12, 1, 21-48. 1941.
199** Kinship in Fiji, *Oc.,* 15, 109-43; 16, 234-53, 297-318. 1945-46.

CATO, A. C.
200** A new religious cult in Fiji, *Oc.*, 18, 146-56. 1947.

CHURCHWARD, C. M.
201* *Tales of a lonely island.* The Oceania Monographs, 4. Sydney (Rotuma). 1939.

COAN, T. M.
202 Love in Fiji, *Putnam's Magazine*, 6, 31-32. 1870.

CORNEY, B. S.
203 *On certain mutilations practised by natives of the Viti islands*, A.A.A.S.R., 2, 646-53. 1890.

COULTER, J. W.
204** Land utilization by Fijians and East Indians in Fiji, Sixth P.S.C.P. 1939, 4, 29-37. 1940.
205** *Fiji, little India of the Pacific.* Chicago. 1942.

CUMMING, C. F. G.
206 Fijian pottery, *Art Journal*, 362. London. 1881.

DEANE, W.
207** Fijian fishing and its superstitions, *Fijian Society, Transactions* 1908-10, 57-61. 1908-10.
208** *Fijian society.* London. 1921.

DERRICK, R. A.
209** *A history of Fiji.* Suva. 1946.
210* *The Fiji islands, a geographical handbook.* Suva. 1951.

FIJIAN SOCIETY
211** *Transactions.* Suva (contains important papers). 1910-24.

FISON, L.
212 Articles and letters on the Fijians (manuscripts). Mitchell Library, Sydney. 1867-73.
213* Notes on Fiji burial customs, *R.A.I.J.*, 10, 137-49. 1880-1a.
214** Land tenure in Fiji, *R.A.I.J.*, 10, 332-52. 1880-1b.
215* *Tales from old Fiji.* London. 1904.

FORBES, L.
216 *Two years in Fiji.* London. 1875.

FORD, C. S.
217** The role of a Fijian chief, *American Sociological Review*, 3, 541-50. 1938.

FOYE, W. G.
218 The Lau islands of Fiji, *G.R.*, 4, 374-86. 1917.

GARDINER, S.
219* The natives of Rotuma, *R.A.I.J.*, 27, 396-435, 457-524. 1898.

GEDDES, W. R.
220** Acceleration of social change in a Fijian community, *Oc.*, 16, 1-14. 1945.
221** *Deuba, a study of a Fijian village.* P.S.M. 22. 1946.

GIFFORD, E. W.
222* Mythology, legends and archaeology in Fiji, *University of California Publications in Semantics and Philology*, 11, 167-77. 1951a.
223** *Archaeological excavations in Fiji*. Anthropological Records 13 : 3, University of California. Berkeley. 1951b.
224** *Tribes of Viti Levu and their origin places. Idem*, 13 : 5.

GORDON, A. C. H.
225 On Fijian poetry, *9th Congress of Orientalists, Transactions*, 2. London. 1893.

GORRIE, J.
226 Fiji as it is, *Royal Colonial Institute, Proceedings*, 160-99. 1882-3.

GOVERNMENT OF FIJI
227* *Report of the 1893 Commission on depopulation*. Suva. 1896.
228* *Report of a Commission on education*. Suva. 1927.
229* *Report of a Commission on education*. Suva. 1945.
230* *Report of the results of the census* . . . 1946. Suva (also reports of other censuses). 1947.
231* Various handbooks of Fiji.

GRIFFIN, A. M.
232 Education of girls in Fiji, *Mid-Pacific*, 47, 4, 349-52. 1934.

HAZLEWOOD, D.
233 Journal (manuscript). Mitchell Library, Sydney. 1844-.

HENDERSON, G. C.
234* *Fiji and the Fijians*. Sydney. 1931.
235 *The discoverers of the Fiji Islands*. London. 1933.

HOCART, A. M.
236* Two Fijian games, *Man*, 9, 108, 184-85. 1909.
237** Fijian customs of Tavua, *R.A.I.J.*, 43, 101-08. 1913a.
238** Heralds in Fiji, *Idem*, 109-13. 1913b.
238a* Totemism in Fiji, *An.*, 9, 727. 1914.
239** The dual organization in Fiji, *Man*, 15, 3, 5-9. 1915a.
240** Rotuman concepts of death, *Man*, 15, 5, 10-12. 1915b.
241** Ethnographical sketch of Fiji, *Man*, 15, 43, 73-77. 1915c.
242* Spirit animals, *Man*, 15, 86, 147-50. 1915d.
243 Early Fijians, *R.A.I.J.*, 49, 42-51. 1919.
244 India and the Pacific, *Ceylon Journal of Science*, Section G, 1, 61-84, 175-78. 1925.
245** *Lau Islands, Fiji*. B.M.B. 62. 1929.

HORNELL, J.
246 The megalithic sea works and temple platforms at Mbau in Fiji, *Man*, 20, 17. 1926.

IM THURN, E.
247* A study of primitive character, *British Association for the Advancement of Science, Report*, 515-24. 1914.

JARRE, R.
248** Mariage et naissance chez les Fidjiens de Kadavu, *S.O.J.*, 2, 79-92. Paris. 1946.

KENNEDY, K.
249* The music system of the Fijians, *Mankind*, 1, 2, 37-39. 1931.

LADD, H. S.
250* Fijians and their sailing canoes, *Asia*, 35, 468-73. 1935.

LA FARGE, J.
251* A Fijian festival, *Century Magazine*, 518-26. 1904.

LAMBERT, S. M.
252** Health survey in Rotuma, *Medical Journal, Australia*, 1. Sydney. 1929.
253** East Indian and Fijian in Fiji, their changing numerical relation. B.M.S.P. 32. 1938.

LANGHAM, F. AND FISON, L.
254 A land appeal case in Fiji, *Fiji Times*, November 29 (reprinted Ovalau, Fiji, 15 pp.) 1880.

LESTER, R. H. (see also under CAPELL, A. and LESTER, R. H.)
255** Notes from Fiji, *Oc.*, 9, 156-69. 1938.
256** Fijian society, *Fiji Society of Science and Industry, Transactions and Proceedings*, 12-22. Suva. 1939-40.
257** Betrothal and marriage customs of Mbau, Fiji, *Oc.*, 10, 273-85. 1940.
257a** Kava drinking in Viti Levu, Fiji, *Oc.*, 12, 97-121. 1942.
258** Effect of war on Fijian society, *Pacific Islands Monthly*, 15, 4, 33-37. 1944.

LIVERSEDGE, A.
259* Vanishing customs in the Fiji islands, *Man*, 21, 81, 133-36. 1921.

LOWIE, R. H.
260 The Fijian collection, *American Museum of Natural History, Journal*, May. 1909.

LYTH, R. B.
261 History of Fiji, daybook, journal, reminiscences, and other papers on Fiji (manuscripts). Mitchell Library, Sydney. 1841-.

MACGREGOR, G.
262** *Ethnological survey of Rotuma and Tokelau islands.* B.M.B. 106. 1932.

McGUSTY, V. W. T.
263** *The decline and recovery of the Fijian race*, Seventh P.S.C.P. New Zealand. 1949.

MACLACHLAN, R. R. C.
264* Native pottery from central and southern Melanesia and western Polynesia, *P.S.J.*, 49, 243-71. 1938.

MANN, C. W.
265* *Education in Fiji.* Australian Council for Educational Research, Publications, 33. Melbourne. 1935.

MARZAN, J. DE
266* Le totémisme aux îles Fiji, *An.*, 2, 400-05. 1907.
266a* Le culte des morts au Fiji, grand île intérieure, *An.*, 4. 1909.

MASON, J. E.
267 On the natives of Fiji, *R.A.I.J.*, 16, 217-20. 1887.

MAUSS, M.
268* L'extension du potlatch en Mélanésie, *l'Anth.* 30, 396-97. 1920.

MILNE, W.
269* On some of the plants used as food by the Feejee islanders, *Botanical Society, Edinburgh, Transactions,* 6, 263-65. 1850.

MOREY, C. J.
270 A modern song of parting, Fiji *P.S.J.*, 42, 106. 1933.

PARHAM, B. E. V.
271** Minor food plants of the Fijian and Indian, *Fiji Society of Science and Industry, Proceedings,* 1940, 12-18. 1940.
272** *Co-operative societies in Fiji.* Seventh P.S.C.P. New Zealand. 1949.

PARHAM, H. B. R.
273** *Fiji plants, their names and uses.* P.S.M., 16. 1939.
273a Traditions and history of Fiji (3 volumes newspaper articles, manuscripts, etc. at Turnbull Library, Wellington). 1944.
274* Folklore and witchcraft in Fiji (typescript, Turnbull Library, Wellington). 1947.

PRITCHARD, W. T.
275 Viti and its inhabitants, *Anthropological Society of London. Memoir,* 1, 195-209. 1863-64.

QUAIN, B.
276** *Flight of the chiefs.* New York. 1942.
277** *Fijian village.* Chicago. (With introduction by R. Benedict analysing Fijian social structure and character.) 1948.

RIVERS, W. H. R.
278* Totemism in Fiji, *Man,* 8, 75, 133-36. 1908.

ROTH, K.
279* Pottery making in Fiji, *R.A.I.J.*, 65, 217-33. 1935.
280* A note on the Fijian "fire-walking" ceremony . . . *Man,* 235. 1936.
281** *Fiji native administration.* Seventh P.S.C.P. New Zealand. 1949.

ROUGIER, E.
282* Danses et jeux aux Fijis, *An.* 6, 466-84 (translated by C. C. Wall, in *Fijian Society, Transactions,* 1915, 16-36). 1911.
283** Diseases and medicines of Fiji, *Fijian Society, Transactions,* 1923, 13-23; 1924, 4-14. (Original French text in *Anthropos,* 2, 1907, 68-79.) 1923-24.

RUSSELL, J.
284** Health education in Fiji: Education of Indians in Fiji, in mimeographed proceedings, *Seminar-Conference on Education in Pacific Countries,* University of Hawaii, Honolulu. 1936.

RUSSELL, W. E.
285* Rotuma, *P.S.J.*, 51, 229-55. 1942.
ST. JOHNSTON, T. R.
286 *The Lau Islands (Fiji) and their fairy tales and folk-lore.* London. 1918.
SCHMIDT, W.
287* Totemism in Fiji, *Man*, 8, 84, 152-53. 1908.
SHEPHERD, G. S.
288 Levuka, *Walkabout*, Dec. 1, 41-43. 1935.
SPENCER, D. M.
289** *Disease, religion and society in the Fiji Islands.* American Ethnological Society Monographs, 2. 1941.
SPENGEL, J. W.
290* Beiträge zur Kenntnis der Fidjische-inseln, *Museum Godeffroy, Journal*, Hamburg, 4, 241-54. 1873.
STANNER, W. E. H.
291** Post-war Fiji: the 1946 census, *Pacific Affairs*, 20, 407-21. 1947.
SURRIDGE, M. N.
292 Decoration of Fiji water-jars, *P.S.J.*, 53, 17-36. 1944.
THOMAS, M. C.
293 Copra-ship voyage to Fiji's outlying islands, *National Geographic Magazine*, July, 121-40. 1950.
THOMPSON, L. M.
294** The culture history of the Lau islands, Fiji, *A.A.*, 40, 181-98. 1938.
295** *Fijian frontier* (Lau Islands.) New York. 1940a.
296** *Southern Lau, an ethnography.* B.M.B. 162. 1940b.
297** The problem of "totemism" in southern Lau, *Oc.*, 17, 211-24. 1947.
298** The relations of men, animals and plants in an island community, Fiji, *A.A.*, 51, 253-67. 1949.
THOMSON, B.
299* The Kalou-vou (ancestor-gods) of the Fijian, *R.A.I.J.*, 24, 340-59. 1895.
300* Concubitancy in the classificatory system of relationship, *R.A.I.J.*, 24, 371-87. 1895.
301** *The Fijians: A study in the decay of custom.* London. 1908.
THOMPSON, J. P.
302* The island of Kadavu, *Scottish Geographical Magazine*, 5, 638-52. 1889.
303 The land of Viti, *Scottish Geographical Magazine*, 10, 120-40. 1894.
304* Fiji: the islands and peoples revisited, *Manchester Geographical Society, Journal*, 48, 31-37. 1937-8.
TONGANIVALU, D.
305* Turtle fishing (Fiji; translated by W. H. Hunter), *Fijian Society, Transactions*, 47-51. 1912-13.
306** Fishing (Fiji; translated by G. A. Beauclerc), *Fijian Society, Transactions*, 7-11. 1914.

307* Canoe building (translated by G. A. Beauclerc), *Fijian Society, Transactions*, 1915, 8-15. 1915.

308** Fiji and the Fijians during the 50 years now ending, 1874-1924 (translated by G. A. Beauclerc), *Fijian Society, Transactions*, 1924, 15-24. 1924.

VAKARURU, H. B.

309* An undiagnosed condition which . . . yields to Fijian medicine, *Native Medical Practitioner*, 2, 4, 360-63. 1937.

VAKATAWA, B. T.

310** What the Fijians believe as the cause of disease, *Native Medical Practitioner*, 3, 522-24. 1940.

WALKER, N.

311 *Fiji. Their people, history and commerce.* London. 1936.

WATERHOUSE, J.

312 *The king and people of Fiji.* London. 1865.

WATI, E. and VULAONO, F. B.

313** A young Fijian mother, *Native Medical Practitioner*, 3, 556-59. 1941.

WHONSBON-ASTON, C. W.

314 *Levuka days of a parson in Polynesia.* London. 1936.

WILHELM, F.

315* Die Fiji Inseln, *Der Erdball*, 3. 1929.

WILKINSON, D.

316 The origin of the Fijian race, *Fiji Times*, December 12, 1908; also *Fijian Society, Transactions*, 1908.

WILLIAMS, T.

317 Journal (manuscript). Mitchell Library, Sydney. 1845-.

WILLIAMS, T. and CALVERT, J.

318 *Fiji and the Fijians.* Vols. 1-2. London. 1858.

WRIGHT, C. H.

319** Varieties of food plants and edible fruits in Fiji, *Fijian Society, Transactions*, 1917.

Tonga

ADAMS, E. H.

320 *Tonga islands and other groups.* London. 1890.

BEAGLEHOLE, E.

321* Tongan colour-vision, *Man*, 39, 170-72. 1939.

322** *Psychic stress in a Tongan village*, Sixth P.S.C.P., 4, 43-52. Berkeley. 1940.

BEAGLEHOLE, E. and P.

323** *Pangai, a village in Tonga.* P.S.M. 18. Wellington. 1941.

BELTRAN Y ROZPIDE, R.

324 Islas Tonga y Samoa, *Sociedad Geografica de Madrid, Boletin*, 13, 153-91. 1882.

BLANC, J. F.
325 *Chez les méridionaux du Pacifique.* Lyon, Paris. 1910.
326* *A history of Tonga, or Friendly islands* (translated from the Tongan by C. S. Ramsay). Vista, California. 1934.
327 *Under the Southern Cross in Tonga Tabu.* Melbourne. 1925.

BROWN, G.
328 Journal and other papers (manuscripts). Mitchell Library, Sydney. 1881-.

BUCK, SIR PETER (TE RANGI HIROA)
329* Material representatives of Tongan and Samoan gods, *P.S.J.*, 44, 48-53, 85-96, 153-62. 1935.
330* Additional wooden images from Tonga, *P.S.J.*, 46, 74-82. 1937.
331* Pan-pipes in Polynesia, *P.S.J.*, 50, 173-84. 1941.

COLLOCOTT, E. E. V.
332 Unpublished manuscripts and papers donated by Mr. Collocott. Mitchell Library, Sydney. 1845-1929.
333** The Supernatural in Tonga, *A.A.*, 23, 415-44. 1921a.
333a** Notes on Tongan religion, *P.S.J.*, 30, 152-63, 227-40. 1921b.
334* *Proverbial sayings of the Tongans,* B.M.O.P., 8, No. 3. 1922a.
335* *Tongan astronomy and the calendar,* B.M.O.P., 8, No. 4. 1922b.
336** Sickness, ghosts and medicine in Tonga, *P.S.J.*, 32, 136-42. 1923.
337* Marriage in Tonga, *P.S.J.*, 32, 221-28. 1923.
338* Kava ceremonial in Tonga, *P.S.J.*, 36, 21-47. 1927.
339* *Tales and poems of Tonga.* B.M.B. 46. 1928.
340** Tonga, yesterday and today, *Mankind,* 2, 134. 1938.

EVA, A.
341** The Tongan midwife: Some native beliefs and surgical procedures encountered in the Tongan group, *Native Medical Practitioner,* 2, 4, 366-67, 383. 1937.

GIFFORD, E. W.
342* *Tongan place names.* B.M.B. 6. 1923.
343* *Tongan myths and tales.* B.M.B. 8. 1924a.
344** Euro-American acculturation in Tonga, *P.S.J.*, 33, 281-92. 1924b.
345** *Tongan society,* B.M.B. 61. 1929.

HALLIDAY, L.
346 Tonga—the friendly isles, *Walkabout,* 16, 5, 18-20. 1950.

HORNELL, J.
347** Outrigger canoes of the Tongan archipelago, *P.S.J.*, 39, 299-309. 1930.

HUNTER, D.
348* The beating and decorating of bark paper in Tonga . . ., in *Primitive papermaking.* London. 1927.

KENNEDY, K.
349* Tongan dance, *Mankind,* July, 44-45. 1931.

G

LUKE, H.
350   Tonga: the last kingdom of the south seas, *Scottish Geographical Magazine*, 59, 2, 49-54. 1943.

LYTH, R. B.
351   Tongan reminiscences, journal, and other papers (manuscript). Mitchell Library, Sydney. 1840-.

McKERN, W. C.
352*   *Archaeology of Tonga.* B.M.B. 60. 1929.
353   Tongan material culture (manuscript, Bishop Museum).

MARINER, W.
354   *An account of the natives of the Tonga Islands* (compiled by John Martin) 2 vols. London. 1817.

MONFAT, A.
355   *Les Tonga ou archipel des amis.* Lyon. 1893.

NEWALL, W. H.
356**   The kava ceremony in Tonga, *P.S.J.*, 56, 364-417. 1947.

RAMSAY, C. S. and PLUMB, C. P.
357   *Tin can island: a story of Tonga.* London. 1939.

REITER, F. X.
358*   *Tongan traditions, Koo Fafagu.* Tongatabu. 1907.
359*   Traditions tonguiennes, *An.*, 2, 230-40, 438-48, 743-54 (1907); 13, 1026-46 (1918); 14, 125-42 (1919). 1907-19.

ST. JOHNSTON, A.
360   *Camping among cannibals* (pp. 1-136). London. 1883.

SHEPHARD, C. Y.
361*   Tonga, *Tropical agriculture*, Trinidad, 22, 160-63. 1945.

SIMKIN, G. G. F.
362*   Modern Tonga, *N.Z.G.*, 1, 99-118. 1945.

SOMERVILLE, H. B. T.
363   *Will Mariner.* London. 1936.

THOMAS, J.
364   History of the Friendly Islands . . . including an account of native customs, beliefs, etc. (manuscript). Mitchell Library, Sydney. 1879.

THOMSON, B.
365*   *Diversions of a Prime Minister.* Edinburgh and London. 1894.
366*   *Savage island: an account of a sojourn in Niue and Tonga.* London. 1902.

THURSTON, J. B.
367   Estimated population in 1870, with comments on decrease (manuscript papers of J. D. Lang, vol. 9, pp. 145-47). Mitchell Library, Sydney. 1870.

VASON, G.
368   *An authentic narrative of four years' residence at Tongataboo* . . . London. 1810.

WEST, T.
369 Ten years in south-central Polynesia: being reminiscences of a personal mission to the Friendly Islands . . . London. 1865.

WHITCOMBE, J. D.
370* Notes on Tongan ethnology, B.M.O.P., 9, 9. 1930.

WILLIAMS, T.
371 Journal and other papers (manuscripts). Mitchell Library, Sydney. 1830-.

WOOD, A. H.
372* History and geography of Tonga. Tongatabu (revised edition). 1938.

Samoa

AA, ROBIDÉ VAN DER
373 Samoa, Société de Géographie de Harlem, Bulletin. 1874.

ADAMS, E. H.
374 Jottings from the Pacific: life and incidents in the Fijian and Samoan islands. London. 1890.

ANDRIESSEN, W. F.
375 Samoa-eilanden. Berlin.

ANONYMOUS
376 Samoan division of time, P.S.J., 37, 228-40. 1928.

BAILEY, T.
377 Samoa, Natural History, 48, 5, 261-71. 1941.

BALLOU, M. M.
378 In old Samoa, Mid-Pacific Magazine, July, 39-44. 1920.

BARSTOW MEMORIAL FOUNDATION
379* Various typescript reports relating to the Feleti School and other activities. 1932-.

BASSETT, H. L.
380 Adventures in Samoa. Los Angeles. 1940.

BASTIAN, A.
381 Einiges aus Samoa . . . Berlin. 1889.

BEAGLEHOLE, E.
382 Trusteeship and New Zealand's Pacific dependencies, P.S.J., 56, 128-57. 1947.

BELTRAN Y ROZPIDE, R.
383 Islas Tonga y Samoa, Sociedad Geografica de Madrid, 13, 153-91. 1882.

BERGER, A.
384* Südseemalanga. Berlin. 1932.

BRIGHAM, W. T.
385* Samoan homes, Mid-Pacific Magazine, 242-46. 1920.

BROWN, G.
386   Journal and other papers (manuscripts). Mitchell Library, Sydney.
      1860-74.

BROWN, G. G.
387* Education in American Samoa; the native teacher in Samoa. Mimeo-
      graphed papers of the *Seminar-Conference on Education in Pacific Countries*,
      University of Hawaii. 1936.

BUCK, P. H. (TE RANGI HIROA)
388** *Samoan material culture*. B.M.B. 75. 1930.
389** Samoan education, *The Friend*, 346-48, 361, 404-06. 1932.
390*   Material representatives of . . . Samoan gods, *P.S.J.*, 44, 48-53, 85-96,
       153-62. 1935.

BÜLOW, W. VON
391* Der Stammbaum der Könige von Samoa, *Globus*, 71, 10, 149-52.
      1897.
392* Die Geschichte des Stammvaters der Samoaner, *Archiv für Ethnographie*,
      11, 6-18. 1898.
393* Zur Besiedlung der Insel Savaii, *Archiv für Ethnographie*, 13, 58-70.
      1901a.
394** Die Nahrungsquellen der Samoaner, *Archiv für Ethnographie*, 13, 185-94.
       1901b.
395** Das Fischereirecht der Eingeborenen von Deutsch-Samoa, *Globus*, 82,
       319-20. 1902.

BURGHOLD, J.
396* Samoanisches Recht, *Der Zeitgeist*, n. 12, Berlin. 1900.

CASTLE, W. M. F.
397   Round about Apia, Samoa, *United Services Institution of New South
      Wales, Journal*, lecture 3. Sydney. 1890.

CHURCHILL, L. P.
398   *Samoa 'Uma*. New York. 1902.

CHURCHILL, W.
399* Sports of the Samoans, *Outing*, March, 562-68. 1899a.
400   Samoan types of beauty (3 pp. seen at Turnbull Library, Wellington.)
      1899b.
401* Samoan kava custom, *Holmes anniversary volume: anthropological essays*.
      Washington. 1916.

CHURCHWARD, W. B.
402   *My consulate in Samoa*. London. 1887.

COOK, P. H.
403** The application of the Rorschach test to a Samoan group, *Rorschach
       Research Exchange*, 6, 2, 51-60. 1942.

COULTER, J. W.
404** *Land utilization in American Samoa*. B.M.B. 170. 1941.

DAVIDSON, J. W.
405** Political development in Western Samoa, *Pacific Affairs*, 136-49. 1948.
DEEKEN, R.
406 *Manuia Samoa: Samoanische Reiseskizzen und Beobachtungen*. Oldenburg. 1901.
DEMANDT, E.
407** Die Fischerei der Samoaner . . ., *Mus. für Völkerkunde, Hamburg, Mitt.* 3, 1. 1913.
DENSMORE, F.
408* The native music of American Samoa, *A.A.*, 34, 415-17. 1932.
DOWNS, E. A.
409 *Daughters of the islands (Samoa)*. Wellington. 1944.
DRUMMOND, S.
410* Canoes and canoe-travelling in Samoa, *Juvenile Missionary Magazine*, 174-75, 194-97. 1873.
DYSON, M.
411 Samoa and the Samoans, *Victorian Review*, 6, 299-311. 1882.
EDUCATION DEPARTMENT, AMERICAN SAMOA
412* Teacher's guide (9 booklets, mimeographed, on Samoan culture, geography, etc.). 1945-47.
ELLA, S.
413 Correspondence and other papers (manuscripts). Mitchell Library, Sydney. 1836-98.
414* The ancient Samoan government, *A.A.A.S.R.*, 6, 596-603. 1895.
EMBREE, E. R.
415* Samoa offers an exchange, *Social Forces*, May. 1933.
EMERSON, A. T.
416* Native craft of Samoa, *U.S. Naval Institute Proceedings*, 60, 381, 1549-52. 1934.
FISHER, V. J.
417** *Ethnobotanical suggestions on potentially useful plant products in . . . Samoa*, 7th P.S.C.P., New Zealand. 1949.
FRASER, J.
418 Samoan story of creation—a "tala", *P.S.J.*, 2, 164-89. 1892.
419* Folk songs and myths from Samoa, *P.S.J.*, 5, 171-83 (1896); 6, 19-36, 67-76, 107-122 (1897); 7, 15-29 (1898); 9, 125-34 (1900).
FREEMAN, J. D.
420* The tradition of Sanalala. Some notes on Samoan folklore, *P.S.J.*, 56, 295-317. 1947.
FREEMAN, L. R.
421 Cricket in Samoa, *Mid-Pacific Magazine*, April, 347-49. 1922.
FRIEDLANDER, B.
422 Notes on the Palolo, *P.S.J.*, 7, 44-46. 1898.
423 *Samoa*. 1899.

GANNIERS, A. DE
423a *Les îles Samoa ou des Navigateurs.* Paris. 1889.

GENTHE, S.
424 *Samoa Reiseschilderungen . . .* Berlin. 1908.

GRAEFFE, E.
425 Samoa oder die Schifferinseln, *Museum Godeffroy, Journal,* 1, 3-32, 75-168; 3, 119-22; 5, 225-40. 1873-6.

GOVERNMENT OF AMERICAN SAMOA
426 *O Le Fa'atonu* (local newspaper, containing various articles on customs). 1947.

GRATTAN, F. J. H.
427** *An introduction to Samoan custom.* Malua (Samoa). 1948.

GREEN, W.
428 Social traits of Samoans, *Applied Sociology, Journal,* November. 1924.

HAMILTON, W. M. and GRANGE, L. I.
429* The soils and agriculture of Western Samoa, *New Zealand Journal of Science and Technology,* 19, 593-624. 1938.

HANDY, E. S. C. and W. C.
430** *Samoan housebuilding, cooking and tattooing.* B.M.B. 15. 1924.

HEIDER, E.
431* *Samoanische Kinderspiele . . .* Sonderdruck der Zeitschrift für Eingeborenen Sprachen, 9, 1. Berlin. 1921.

HESSE-WARTEGG, E. VON
432 *Samoa, Bismarckarchipel, und Neuguinea . . .* Leipzig. 1902.

HOOD, J.
433 The women of Samoa, *Goththwaite's Geographical Magazine,* February, 113-18. 1910.

HORNELL, J.
434* *String figures of Fiji and western Polynesia.* B.M.B. 39. 1927.

HOUZE, E.
435* Les Samoans de Leone (Ile Tutuila), *Société d' Anthropologie de Bruxelles,* 8. 1899-1900.

JORDAN, D. S. and KELLOGG, V. L.
436 Tutuila (U.S.), *Atlantic Monthly,* 207-17. 1904.

KEESING, F. M.
437** Language change in relation to native education in Samoa, *Mid-Pacific Magazine,* 44, 303-13. 1932.
438** *Modern Samoa.* London and Stanford. 1934.
439** The taupo system of Samoa—a study in institutional change, *Oc.,* 8, 1-14. 1938.

KOLKINSKI, M.
440* Die Musik der Primitivstämme auf Malaka und ihre Beziehungen zur Samoanischen Musik, *An.,* 25, 585-648. 1930.

KRÄMER, A.
441** *Die Samoa-Inseln.* Vols. 1-2. Stuttgart. 1902-03.
442* *Hawaii, Ostmikronesien und Samoa* . . . Stuttgart. 1906.
443* *Salamasina: Bilder aus altsamoanischer Kultur und Geschichte.* Stuttgart. 1923.

KURESA, IELU
444** Samoan customs and the cost of surgery to the natives, *Native Medical Practitioner*, 2, 197-207. 1935.

KURZE, G.
445 *Samoa, Das Land, die Leute und die Mission.* Berlin. 1900.

LESSON, P. A.
446 *Traditions des îles Samoa.* Paris. 1876.

LEWIS, A. M.
447* *They call them savages.* London. 1938.

LONDON MISSIONARY SOCIETY
448* *O le tusi fa'alupega o Samoa.* Malua (Samoa). 1946.

McKAY, C. G. R.
449* *A chronology of Western Samoa.* Apia. 1937.

MARQUARDT, C.
450* *Die Tätowirung beider Geschlechter in Samoa.* Berlin. 1899.
451* *Verzeichniss einer ethnologischen Sammlung aus Samoa.* Berlin. 1902.

MARQUES, A.
452 Notes pour servir à une monographie des îles Samoa, *Sociedade de Geographia, Lisboa, Boletin*, 8, 1-2. 1888-89.
453 *Iles Samoa.* Lisbon. 1889.

MATAGI, S.
454** Methods, treatment and superstitions of Samoan medicine men and midwives relative to pregnancy and parturition and medical care, *O Le Fa'atonu*, 45, 6, 1. 1948.

MEAD, M.
455** *Coming of age in Samoa.* London and New York. 1928a.
456** The role of the individual in Samoan culture, *R.A.I.J.*, 58, 481-96. 1928b.
457** *Social organization of Manua.* B.M.B. 76. 1930.
458** Samoans, in *Co-operation and competition among primitive peoples*, 282-312. 1937.

MIDKIFF, F. E.
459 A charitable trust makes plans to serve a primitive people, *Mid-Pacific Magazine*, 45, 17-29. 1933.

MONFAT, A.
460 *Les îles Samoa ou archipel des Navigateurs.* Lyon. 1890.

NELSON, O. F.
461* Legends of Samoa, *P.S.J.*, 34, 124-45. 1925.

NEW ZEALAND GOVERNMENT
462   *Royal Commission on Western Samoa, Report*. Wellington. 1927.

NORTH, V.
463   There were clouds on Vaiomanu, *Mid-Pacific Magazine*, 47, 7, 517-22. 1934.

PENISIMANI
464   Samoan stories, proverbs, sayings, etc. (manuscript). Mitchell Library, Sydney. 1865-70.

POWELL, T.
465*   Some folk-songs and myths from Samoa, translated by T. Powell and G. Pratt . . ., *Journal Royal Society of New South Wales*, 24, 195-217 (1890); 25, 241-86 (1891); 26, 264-301 (1892); 29, 366-93 (1895). 1890-95.

PRATT, G.
466   The genealogy of the sun—a Samoan legend, *A.A.A.S.R.*, 1, 447-63. 1888.
467*   Genealogy of kings and princes of Samoa, *A.A.A.S.R.*, 2, 655-63. 1890.

PRITCHARD, W. T.
468   *Polynesian reminiscences*. London. 1866.

REINECKE, F.
469*   Die Samoaner und die Kokospalme, *Globus*, 75, 227-30. 1889.
470*   Anthropologische Aufnahmen und Untersuchungen, ausgefuhrt auf den Samoa-inseln 1894-95 . . ., *Z.E.*, 28, 101-45. 1896.
471*   Zur Kennzeichnung der Verhältnisse auf den Samoa-inseln, *Globus*, 76, 4-13. 1899.
472*   Betrachtungen über die Samoanische Schöpfungsgeschichte. *Zeitschrift für Afrik. und Ozean. Sprachen*. 282-88. 1900.
473*   *Samoa*. Berlin. 1902.
474   Savaii, *Petermann's Mitt.*, 49, 1-11. 1903.

RIEDEL, O.
475*   *Der kampf um Deutsch-Samoa*. Berlin. 1938.

RITCHIE, T. R.
476*   Diet, *Medical Journal of Australia, Supplement*, Sept. 10. 1927.

RUTHERFORD, D. A. J.
477*   Education in Western Samoa, in *The Maori and education*, edited by Jackson, P. M. Wellington. 1931.

SAFFORD, W. E.
478*   Old and new Samoa, *A.A.*, 23, 498-501. 1921.

SCHEURMANN, E.
479*   *Samoa: ein Bilderwerk*. Konstanz. (Excellent photographs). 1926.

SCHMIDT, R.
480*   Die Samoa-inseln, *Deutschlands Kolonien*, 2, 413-29. 1902.

SCHULTZ-EWERTH, E. VON
481   Samoan version of the story of Apakura, *P.S.J.*, 18, 139-42. 1909.

482** The most important principles of Samoan family law, and the laws of inheritance, *P.S.J.*, 20, 43-53. 1911.
483* *Erinnerungen an Samoa*. Berlin. 1926.
484* Proverbial expressions of the Samoans (translated by Brother Herman), *P.S.J.*, 58, 4, 139-84; 59, 1, 35-62. 1949-50.

SETCHELL, W. A.
485* *American Samoa: Part II. Ethnobotany of the Samoans*. Carnegie Institution, Department of Marine Biology, Publication 341. 1924.

SIERICH, O.
486* Samoanische Märchen, *Archiv für Ethnographie*, 13, 223-37; 14, 15-23; 15, 167-200; 16, 88-110; 17, 182-88. 1900-05.

SMITH, I. E.
487 Peace and war in Samoa, *Centennial Magazine*, 1, 579-85, 639-51, 723-30, 821-27, 862-68. 1888-9.

SMITH, S. P.
488* Kava drinking ceremonies among the Samoans . . ., *P.S.J.*, 29, Supplement, 1-21. 1920.

STAIR, J. B.
489 Samoa; whence peopled? *P.S.J.*, 4, 47-58. 1895.
490* Mythology and spirit-lore of old Samoa, *P.S.J.*, 5, 33-57. 1896.
491* *Old Samoa*. London. 1897a.
492* Palolo, a sea worm eaten by the Samoans, *P.S.J.*, 6, 141-44. 1897b.
493 Names and movements of the heavenly bodies as looked at from a Samoan point of view, *P.S.J.*, 7, 48-49. 1898.

STOKES, J. F. G.
494* *Fish-poisoning in Samoa*, B.M.O.P., 7, 10, 229-33. 1921.

STEVENSON, R. L.
495 *A footnote to history*. New York. 1892.

STUEBEL, O.
496 *Samoanische texte . . . Veröffentlichungen aus dem Königlichen Museum für Völkerkunde, IV*, 2-4. Berlin. 1896.

SU'A, K.
497 Education in American Samoa, two papers in *Proceedings, First Pan-Pacific Conference on Education*. Honolulu. 1927.

TATTERSALL, A. J.
498 *Ansichten von Samoa, herausgegeben vom Verkehrsverein Apia*. Apia.

TENNENT, H. C.
499 Samoa: old and new, *Hawaiian Historical Society, Annual Report*, 35, 17-31. 1926.

THILENIUS, G.
500** Bonito- und Haifang in Alt-Samoa, *Globus*, 78, 127-28. 1900.
501** Die Fahrzeuge der Samoaner, *Globus*, 80, 167-73. 1901.

THOMSON, A.
502 Samoan head-shaping, *P.S.J.*, 37, 369-71. 1928.

TOGAMAU, FAATIGA
503** Infant feeding in native villages (Samoa), *Native Medical Practitioner*, 2, 255-62. 1935.
503a** Preparation and use of niutolo and suau'u manogi oils (coconut oils), *Idem*, 3, 2, 503-05. 1940.

TREGEAR, E.
504   Ceremonial language (Samoa), *New Zealand Institute, Transactions*, 27, 593-97. 1895.

TROOST, E.
505   *Samoanische Eindrucke und Betrachtungen*. Berlin. 1901.

TUIAVII
506   *Der Papalaji: die Veden des Südseehäuptlings Tuiavii aus Tiavea*. 1922.

TUITELEAPAGA, N. A. and others
507* The fight against "bush" medicine . . ., *O Le Fa'atonu* (American Samoa), 45, 5, 1-2. 1948.

TURNER, F. M.
508   Sport in Samoan craft, *Outing*, October 17-21. 1894.

TURNER, G.
509* *Samoa a hundred years ago and long before*. London. 1884.

TURVALE, T.
510   History of modern Samoa (unpublished manuscript translated from the Samoan by E. Riddel, Samoan Affairs Office, Apia). 1918.

UNITED NATIONS
511** *The population of Western Samoa*. Department of Social Affairs, Reports on the Population of Trust Territories, 1. Lake Success. 1948.

WATSON, R. W.
512   *History of Samoa*. Wellington. 1918.

WIST, B. O.
513* Ethnology as a basis for education, *Social Science*, October, 336-47. 1935.

WOERL, L.
514   *Samoa—Land und Leute*. Leipzig. 1901.

Tokelaus

BOISSE, E.
515   Les îles Samoa, Nuku-Nono, Fakaofo, Wallis et Hoorn, *Société de Géographie, Bulletin* 6, 10, 428-39. 1875.

BURROWS, W.
516* Some notes and legends of a south sea island. Fakaofo of the Tokelau or Union Group, *P.S.J.*, 32, 143-73. 1923.

HALE, H.
517   Ethnography and philology, *Narrative of the United States Exploring Expedition*, 6. Philadelphia. 1846.

LISTER, J. T.
518* Notes on the natives of Fakaofo (Bowditch Island) Union Group, R.A.I.J., 2, 43-63. 1891.

MACGREGOR, G.
519** Ethnological survey of Rotuma and Tokelau Islands. B.M.B. 106, 34-37. 1932.
520** Ethnology of Tokelau Islands, B.M.B. 146. 1937.

NEWELL, J. E.
521* Notes, chiefly ethnological, of the Tokelau, Ellice, and Gilbert Islands, A.A.A.S.R., 6, 603-07. 1895.

SMITH, S. P.
522** A note on the Tokelau or Union Group, P.S.J., 31, 91-93. 1922.

TUTUILA
523 The Line islanders . . . Notes on the races known as the Tokelaus . . ., P.S.J., 1, 263-72. 1892.

Gilbert and Ellice Islands
BINGHAM, H.
524 The Gilbert islanders, Pacific Commercial Advertiser, Supplement, April 24. 1880.

BURNETT, F.
525 Through tropic seas, 62-139. London. 1910.

DAVID, E.
526 Funafuti. London. 1899.

DICKEY, L. A.
527* String figures from . . . Gilbert islands. B.M.B. 54. 1928.

DREWS, R. A.
528** Gilbert Islands horticulture: the babai, A.A., 46, 571-72. 1944.
529** Some Gilbert Island fish traps, Idem, 47, 171-73. 1945a.
530** Gilbert Island canoe, Idem, 47, 471-74. 1945b.
531** Notes on Gilbert Islands houses and house construction, Idem, 48, 284-89. 1946.

ELLIS, A. F.
532* Ocean Island and Nauru. Sydney (2nd edition). 1936.
533 Mid-Pacific outposts. Auckland. 1946.

FINSCH, O.
534** Ethnologische Erfahrungen und Belegstücke aus der Südsee. Dritte Abt: Mikronesien (West-ozeanien), 1. Gilberts-inseln, Ann. Naturhist. Mus., Wien, 8, 1-106, 417-18. 1893.

GRIMBLE, A. F.
535* Canoe crests of the Gilbert islanders, Man, 21, 49, 81-85. 1921a.
536** From birth to death in the Gilbert Islands, R.A.I.J., 51, 25-54. 1921b.
537* Myths from the Gilbert Islands, Folk-Lore Journal, Jan.-June, 91-112. 1922.

538** Canoes in the Gilbert islands. *R.A.I.J.*, 54, 101-39. 1924.
539** Gilbertese astronomy, *P.S.J.*, 40, 197-224. 1931.
540** *Migrations of a Pandanus people.* P.S.M., 12. 1933-34.
541* War finds its way to Gilbert Islands, *National Geographic Magazine*, 83, 71-92. 1943.
542* Fishing for man-eating sharks, *Clipper Travel*, April, 18-20. 1950.

GRUBE, A. W.

543   Aus den . . . Gilbertinseln, in *Bilder und Szenen aus Australien und Ozeanien*, 10th edition. Stuttgart. 1926.

HAGER, C.

544   *Die Marshall-inseln in Erd- und Völkerkunde, handel und Mission. Mit einem Anhang: die Gilbert-inseln.* Leipzig. 1889.

HARTZER, F.

545   *Les îles blanches des mers du sud. Histoire du vicariat apostolique des archipels Gilbert et Ellice.* Paris. 1900.

HEDLEY, C.

546** *The ethnology of Funafuti.* Australian Museum, Memoir 3, 227-304. 1897.

HICKING, A.

547** Foodstuffs in the Gilbert Islands, *Native Medical Practitioner*, 3, 1, 432-37. 1939.

HILDER, B.

548   We went recruiting in the Gilberts, *Pacific Islands Monthly*, 19, 7, 44-58. 1949.
549   King Neptune's children, *Walkabout*, 16, 6, 18-20. 1950.

KENNEDY, D. G.

550** *Field notes on the culture of Vaitupu, Ellice Islands.* P.S.M., 9. 1931.

KRÄMER, A.

551** *Hawaii, Ostmikronesien und Samoa* . . . Stuttgart, 253-361, 441-57. 1906.

LAMBERT, S. M.

552** *Health survey of the Gilbert and Ellice Islands.* Suva. 1924.

LUOMALA, K.

553** *Plants of the Gilbert Islands* (B.M.B., in press); Ethnography of the Gilbert Islands (in preparation).

McCALLUM, T. M.

554   *Adrift in the South Seas* (pp. 247-85). London. 1934.

MARSHALL, W. H.

555   *Report on Ellice, Gilbert . . . Islands.* Sydney. 1881.

MAUDE, H. E.

556** Culture change and education in the Gilbert and Ellice islands, mimeographed proceedings, *Seminar-Conference on Education in Pacific Countries.* University of Hawaii, Honolulu. 1936.
557** The co-operative movement in the Gilbert and Ellice Islands, Seventh P.S.C.P., 1948. Auckland. 1950a.
558** Social development in the south Pacific, *South Pacific*, 4, 5, 73-77. 1950b.

MAUDE, H. E. and H. C.
559** Adoption in the Gilbert islands, *P.S.J.*, 40, 225-35. 1931.
560** Social organization of Banaba or Ocean Island, central Pacific, *Idem*,
    41, 262-301. 1932.
MOORE, W. R.
561 Gilbert Islands in the wake of battle, *National Geographic Magazine*, 87,
    2, 129-62. 1945.
MURDOCH, G. M.
562 Gilbert Islands weapons and armour, *P.S.J.*, 31, 174-75. 1923.
NEWELL, J. E.
563* Notes, chiefly ethnological, of the Tokelau, Ellice, and Gilbert islanders,
    A.A.A.S.R., 6, 603-10, Brisbane. 1895.
O'BRIEN, S.
564* How an Ellice Island baby is fed if its mother cannot breast-feed it,
    Native Medical Practitioner, 3, 559-61. 1941.
PARKINSON, R.
565* Beiträge zur Ethnographie der Gilbert Insulaner, *Internationales Archiv
    für Ethnographie*, II, 31-48, 90-106. 1889.
POPE, H. B.
566* Nauru and Ocean Island, *Journal of Agriculture*, Victoria, Australia,
    August 1921; March, November, 1922. 1921-22.
SEURAT, L. G.
567* Sur quelques similitudes des . . . coutumes des indigènes de Funafuti
    (Ellice Group) et des indigènes des îles de la Société, et l'archipel des
    Tuamotus . . ., *Linnean Society of New South Wales, Proceedings*, 28,
    926-31. 1903.
SHEPHARD, C. Y.
568* Gilbert and Ellice Islands, *Tropical Agriculture*, Trinidad, 22, 179-83.
    1945.
SMITH, S. P.
569 The first inhabitants of the Ellice group, *P.S.J.*, 5, 209-10. 1896.
SPOEHR, A.
570** The generation type kinship system in the Marshall and Gilbert Islands,
    Southwestern Journal of Anthropology, 5, 107-16. 1949.
STEVENSON, R. L.
571 *In the south seas.* London. 1890.
TUTUILA
572 The Line Islanders . . . Notes on the races known as the Tokelaus . . .,
    P.S.J., 263-72. 1892.
WALCOTT, A. M.
573 *Ray-skin rasps*, B.M.O.P., 1,2, 32-33. 1900.
WHITMEE, S. J.
574 The ethnology of Polynesia, *R.A.I.J.*, 8, 261-75. 1879.

WOODFORD, C. M.
575* The Gilbert Islands, G.J., 6, 325-50. 1895.

Nauru

DAKIN, W. J.
576 The story of Nauru, *Walkabout*, 1, 5, 33-36. 1935.

DELAPORTE, P. H.
577 Nauru as it was, and as it is now, *The Friend* (Honolulu), June, 6-7; July, 13-14; August, 7-8; September, 9-11. 1907.

EARLE, R. V.
578* The bird catchers of Nauru, *Walkabout*, 7, 11, 20. 1941.

ELLIS, A. F.
579* *Ocean Island and Nauru.* Sydney (2nd edition). 1936.
580* *Mid-Pacific outposts.* Auckland. 1946.

HAMBRUCH, P.
581** *Nauru. Ergebnisse der Südsee-Expedition* 1908-1910, II: *Ethnographie*, Bd.1, *Halbbände* 1,2. Hamburg. 1914-15.

KAYSER, P. A.
582** Die Eingeborenen von Nauru, *An.*, 12-13, 313-37. Vienna. 1917-18.
583** Spiel und Sport auf Náoero, *Idem*, 16-17, 681-711; 18-19, 297-328. 1921-24.
584** Der Pandanus auf Nauru, *Idem*, 29, 775-91. 1934.
585** Die Fischerei auf Nauru (Pleasant Island), *Mitt. Anthropologischen Gesellschaft, Wien*, 66, 92-131, 149-204. 1936.

KRÄMER, A.
586* Nauru, *Globus*, 74, 10, 153-58. 1898.

MOSS, F. J.
587 *Through atolls and islands in the great south sea.* London. 1886.

POPE, H. B.
588* Nauru and Ocean Island, *Journal of Agriculture*, Victoria, Australia, August 1921; March, November 1922.

RHONE, R. D.
589 Nauru, the richest island in the south seas, *National Geographic Magazine*, 40, 559-89. 1921.

STEPHEN, E.
590** Note on Nauru, *Oc.*, 7, 34-63. 1936.

WEDGWOOD, C. H.
591** Report on research work in Nauru Island, Central Pacific, *Oc.*, 6 359-91; 7, 1-33. 1936.

Wallis (Uvea) and Horne (Hoorn, Futuna)

BATAILLON, P.
592 *Langue d'Uvea.* Paris. 1932.

BLANC, J. M.
593* Les îles Wallis. Paris. 1914.
BOISSE, E.
594 Les îles Samoa, Nuku-Nono, Fakaofo, Wallis et Hoorn, Société de Géographie, Bulletin 6, 10, 428-39. 1875.
BURROWS, E. G.
595** Ethnology of Futuna. B.M.B. 138. 1936.
596** Ethnology of Uvea (Wallis Island). B.M.B. 145. 1937.
597** Topography and culture on two Polynesian islands, G.R., 28, 214-23. 1938.
598** Songs of Uvea and Futuna. B.M.B. 183. 1945.
LEVERD, A.
599* Etude linguistique et ethnographique sur l'île Uvea, S.E.O.B., 2, 94-103. 1917.
SMITH, S. P.
600* Futuna, or Horne Island and its people, P.S.J., 1, 33-52. 1892.
VIALA, M.
601** Les îles Wallis et Horn, Société Neuchâteloise de Géographie, Bulletin 28, 209-86. 1919.

Cook Islands

ADAMS, E. H.
602 Tonga islands and other groups. London. 1890.
BEAGLEHOLE, E. & P.
603** Ethnology of Pukapuka. B.M.B. 150. 1938.
604** Brief Pukapukan case history, P.S.J., 48, 144-55. 1939.
605** Personality development in Pukapukan children, in Language, Culture, and Personality: Essays in memory of Edward Sapir (ed. by Leslie Spier and others). Menasha, Wisconsin. 1941.
606** Islands of danger. Wellington. 1944.
607 Trusteeship and New Zealand's Pacific dependencies, P.S.J., 56, 128-57. 1947.
608** Social and political changes in the Cook Islands, Pacific Affairs, 21, 383-98. 1948.
BELTRAN Y ROZPIDE, R.
609 Las islas Cook y Tubuai . . ., Sociedad Geografica de Madrid, 15, 326-37. 1883.
BROWNE, A. H.
610 An account of some early ancestors of Rarotonga, P.S.J., 6, 1-10. 1897.
BUCK, P. H. (TE RANGI HIROA)
611* Aitutaki moko: some tattoo patterns . . ., Dominion Museum Bulletin 3, 98. 1911.
612** The material culture of the Cook Islands (Aitutaki). Board of Maori Ethnological Research, Memoir 1. New Plymouth. 1927.
613* Fish poisoning in Rarotonga, P.S.J., 37, 57-66. 1928.

614** *Ethnology of Tongareva.* B.M.B. 92. 1932a.
615** *Ethnology of Manihiki-Rakahanga.* B.M.B. 99. 1932b.
616** *Mangaian society.* B.M.B. 122. 1934.
617** *Arts and crafts of the Cook Islands.* B.M.B. 179. 1944.

BUZACOTT, A.
618   Diary, journal and other papers (manuscripts). Mitchell Library, Sydney. 1832-.

CAMPBELL, J. D.
619*   The "paru matau" of Rarotonga, *Mankind*, 1, 112-14. 1932.

DAVIS, T. R. A.
620** Rarotonga today, *P.S.J.*, 56, 197-218. 1947.

EMORY, K. P.
621*   Manihiki inlaid bowls, *Ethnologia Cranmorensis*, 4, 20-26. 1939.

FISHER, V. J.
622** *Ethno-botanical suggestions on potentially useful plant products in the Cook Islands* . . ., Seventh P.S.C.P. New Zealand. 1949.

GILL, W. W.
623*   *Life in the southern islands.* London. 1876.
624*   *Historical sketches of savage life in Polynesia.* Wellington. 1880.
625   *From darkness to light in Polynesia.* London. 1894a.
626*   Mangaia (Hervey Islands), *A.A.A.S.R.*, 2, 323-53. 1894b.
627   A word about the original inhabitants of Pukapuka Island, *P.S.J.*, 21, 120-24. 1912.
628   The origin of the island of Manihiki, *P.S.J.*, 24, 144-51. 1915.
629*   *Rarotongan records, being extracts from the papers of the late Rev. W. Wyatt Gill.* New Plymouth. 1916.

GOLD, E.
630*   The birth ropes of Mangaia and some superstitions, *P.S.J.*, 54. 1945.

GOSSET, R. W. G.
631   Notes on the discovery of Rarotonga, *A.G.*, 3, 8, 4-15. 1940.

GRUNING, E. L.
632*   Notes on burial caves in the Cook group, South Pacific, *Ethnologia Cranmorensis*, 1, 21-25. 1937.

GUDGEON, W. E.
633*   Phallic emblems from Atiu Islands, *P.S.J.*, 13, 210-12. 1904.
634*   The origin of the ta-tatau or heraldic marks at Aitutaki Island, *P.S.J.*, 14, 217-18. 1907.

HICKLING, H. H.
635** Notes on the adoption and naming of children in Mangaia, *P.S.J.*, 54, 83-86. 1945.

LAMBERT, S. M.
636** *Health survey of the Cook Islands.* Wellington. 1926.
637** Some Polynesian medical superstitions encountered in the Cook Islands, *Journal of Tropical Medicine and Hygiene*, July 1, 6 pp. 1933.

LARGE, J. T.
638* Some notes on Atiu Island, Cook group, South Pacific, P.S.J., 22, 67-76. 1913.

Low, D.
639** Birth and allied customs in Aitutaki, P.S.J., 52, 199-201. 1943.

MACGREGOR, G.
640** Notes on the ethnology of Pukapuka, B.M.O.P., 11, 6. 1935.

MOSS, F. J.
641* The Maori polity in the island of Rarotonga, P.S.J., 3, 20-26. 1894.

NICHOLAS, H.
642* Genealogies and historical notes from Rarotonga, parts I-III, P.S.J. 1, 20-29, 65-75; 2, 271-79. 1892-93.

NORDHOFF, C. B.
643** Fishing for the oil fish (Ruvettus) . . . at Atiu, Hervey group, and elsewhere . . ., Natural History, 28, 40-45. 1928.

NUMA, J.
644* Penrhyn island, The Native Medical Practitioner, 3, 1, 415-16. 1939.

OLDMAN, W. O.
645* Oldman collection of Polynesian artifacts, Tahiti, Austral and Cook Islands. P.S.M. 15. 1938-40.

PAKOTI, J.
646 The first inhabitants of Aitutaki (translated by H. Nicholas), P.S.J., 4, 59-70. 1895.

PITMAN, C.
647 Journal (manuscript). Mitchell Library, Sydney. 1827-42.

READ, C. H.
648* On the origin and sacred character of certain ornaments in the S.E. Pacific, R.A.I.J., 21, 139-59. 1892.

SKINNER, H. D.
649* Notes on pearl shell pendants in the Cook Islands, P.S.J., 44, 187-89. 1935.

SMITH, S. P.
650* Tongareva, or Penrhyn island, and its people, New Zealand Institute Transactions and Proceedings, 22, 85-103. 1889.

STERNDALE, H. B.
651* A lonely land . . ., Monthly Review (Wellington), 195-204, 269-79, 346-55, 384-92, 435-43. 1890.

TE-ARIKI-TARA-ARE
652** History and traditions of Rarotonga, P.S.J., 8, 61-88 (1899); 24, 178-98 (1918); 28, 55-78, 134-51, 183-208 (1919); 29, 1-19, 45-69, 107-127, 165-88 (1920); 30, 1-15, 54-70, 129-41, 201-26 (1921).

WALLACE, W. D.
653* Notes on Manihiki island, P.S.J., 20, 222-23. 1920.

H

Niue

BUCK, P. H. (TE RANGI HIROA)
654* Some notes on the small outrigger canoe of Niue Fekai, *Dominion Museum, Bulletin* 3, 91-94. Wellington. 1911.

CHURCHILL, W.
655* Niue: a reconnaissance, *American Geographic Society, Bulletin*, 151-56. 1908.

FISHER, V. J.
656** *Ethno-botanical suggestions on potentially useful plants in the Cook islands, Niue, and Samoa,* Seventh P.S.C.P., New Zealand. 1949.

GILL, W.
657 *Gems from the coral islands. Vol. II: Eastern Polynesia.* London. 1856.

LAWES, W. G.
658 Journal and letter-book (manuscripts). Mitchell Library, Sydney. 1863-70.

LOEB, E. M.
659** The shaman of Niue, *A.A.*, 26, 393-402. 1924.
660** *History and traditions of Niue.* B.M.B. 32, 1926. 1926.

SMITH, S. P.
661* Niue island and its people, *P.S.J.*, 11, 80-106, 163-78, 195-218; 12, 1-31, 85-119. 1902-03.

THOMSON, B.
662* *Savage island: an account of a sojourn in Niue and Tonga.* London. 1902.

Societies

ADAMS, H. (ed.)
663* *Memoirs of Arii Taimai.* Paris. 1901.

AHNNE, E.
664* Allocution de M. Ahnne, président de la S.E.O. (Tahitian beliefs) *S.E.O.B.*, 5, 666-71. 1936.

AGOSTINI, J.
665* *Folk-lore de Tahiti et des îles voisines. Changements survenus dans les coutumes, moeurs . . .,* Revue des Traditions Populaires, 15, 2-3. 1900.

ALCAN, E.
666 *Les cannibales et leur temps: souvenirs de la campagne de l'Océanie sous le commandant Marceau . . .* Paris. 1887.

BELTRAN Y ROZPIDE, R.
667 Las islas Tahiti, *Sociedad Geografica de Madrid, Boletin,* 13, 247-60, 373-87; 14, 39-60, 92-109, 151-74. 1882-83.

BENOÎT, P.
668 *Océanie française.* Paris. 1933.

BERTRANA, A.
669 *Fenua Tahiti: vision de Polynésie.* Neuchâtel. 1943.

BEST, E.
670* Some place names of islands in the Society group, *P.S.J.*, 26, 111-15. 1917.
BOLTON, W. W.
671* The beginnings of Papeete . . ., *S.E.O.B.*, 5, 437-42. 1935.
672* Pomares of Tahiti and the heraldic law, *Pacific Islands Monthly*, 9, 5, 38-39. 1938.
BOVIS, E. DE
673 *Etat de la société Taitienne à l'arrivée des Européens* (from *Revue Coloniale*, 1855). Papeete. 1909.
BRIGHAM, W. T.
674* Marquesan and Tahitian homes, *Mid-Pacific Magazine*, October, 393-96. 1916.
BOUGE, L. J.
675* *Notes on Polynesian pounders*, B.M.O.P., 9, No. 2. 1930.
BUCK, P. H. (TE RANGI HIROA)
676* Canoe outrigger-attachments in Tahiti and New Zealand, *P.S.J.*, 38, 183-215. 1929.
677* The feather cloak of Tahiti, *P.S.J.*, 52, 12-15, 100. 1943.
BUNZENDAHL, O.
678* Uber sportliche Kämpfe und gymnastische Spiele in Alt-Tahiti, *Veröffentlichungen aus dem Deutschen Kolonial- und Uebersee-Museum in Bremen*, 1, 2, 279-303. 1935a.
679* *Tahiti und Europa*, I . . . Studien zur Völkerkunde, 8. Leipzig. 1935b.
BURCHETT, W. G.
680 New ways of fishing . . ., *Pacific Islands Monthly*, 10, 10, 38-40. 1940.
CAILLOT, A-C. E.
681* *Les Polynésiens orientaux au contact de la civilisation*. Paris. 1909.
CALDERON, G. (TIHOTI)
682 *Tahiti*. London. 1921.
CANDACE, G.
683 Les établissements français de l'Océanie, *Revue du Pacifique*, 4, 598-615. 1925.
CHADOURNE, M. and GUIERRE, M.
684* *Marehurehu:entre le jour et la nuit: croyances, légendes, coutumes et textes poétiques* . . . Paris. 1925.
CHAUVEL, C.
685 Tahiti today, *Walkabout*, 1, 1, 35-38. 1934.
CHEESMAN, L. E.
686 *Isles near the sun*. London. 1927.
CHESNEAU, J.
687* Histoire de Huahine et autres îles Sous-le-Vent, *S.E.O.B.*, 25, 57-67; 26, 81-98. 1928.

106   SOCIAL ANTHROPOLOGY IN POLYNESIA

COMMISSARIAT GÉNÉRAL DES ÉTABLISSEMENTS FRANÇAIS DE l'OCÉANIE.
688   Dans les eaux du Pacifique. Exposition Coloniale Internationale. 2 vols.
       Paris. 1931.
CRAMPTON, H. E.
689*   The songs of Tahiti, American Museum of Natural History, Journal,
       12, 4, 141-44. 1912.
CHRISTIAN, F. W.
690*   Eastern Pacific lands: Tahiti and the Marquesas. London. 1910.
CROSSLAND, C.
691*   The island of Tahiti, G. J., 71, 561-85. 1928.
CUMMING, C. F. G.
692   The last king of Tahiti, Contemporary Review, 41, 821-36. 1882.
CURTON, E. DE
693   Tahiti: terre française combattante. Publications de la France Combattante.
       London. 1942.
694   Tahiti and French Polynesia. London. 1943.
CUZENT, G.
695   Iles de la Société. Tahiti. 1860.
ELLIS, W.
696   Polynesian researches. Vols. 1, 2. London. 1829.
EMORY, K. P.
697*   L'art Tahitien, S.E.O.B., 19. 1927.
698*   Stone remains of the Society Islands. B.M.B. 116. 1933.
FERDINAND-LOP, S.
699   Les possessions françaises du Pacifique. Paris. 1933.
FREEMAN, L. R.
700*   Song and dance in Tahiti, Overland Monthly, January. 1915.
GAUSSIN, L.
701   Cosmogonie tahitienne, Le Tour du Monde, 10-12, 302-04. Paris. 1860.
GIBBINGS, R.
702   Iorana! a Tahitian journal. London. 1932.
GUILD, C.
703   Rainbow in Tahiti. New York. 1948.
GUILLOT, F.
704   Souvenirs d'un colonial en Océanie. Taiti . . . (1888-1911). Annecy. 1935.
GUIZOT, M.
705   Les îles Marquises et Taiti, Mémoires pour servir à l'histoire de mon temps,
       7, 40-117. Paris. 1871.
HALL, J. N.
706   Under the south. London. 1928.
HALL, J. N. and NORDHOFF, C. B.
707   Faery lands of the south seas. New York. 1921.

HANDY, E. S. C.
708** *History and culture in the Society Islands.* B.M.B. 79. 1931.
709** *Houses, boats and fishing in the Society Islands.* B.M.B. 90. 1932.
HANDY, W. C.
710* *String figures from the Marquesas and Society Islands.* B.M.B. 18. 1925.
711** *Handicrafts of the Society Islands.* B.M.B. 42. 1927.
HASSALL, R.
712 Collection of correspondence and other papers, including writings of Revs. Crook, Nott, Orsmond, Henry, and other missionaries (manuscripts). Mitchell Library, Sydney.
HENRY, T.
713* Te umu-ti, a Raiatean ceremony, *P.S.J.*, 2, 105-08. 1893.
714 The legend of Honoura, *P.S.J.*, 4, 256-94. 1895.
715* Tahitian folklore compared with the Samoan and Hawaiian, *Hawaiian Historical Society, Annual Reports*, 5. 1897.
716** *Ancient Tahiti.* B.M.B. 48. 1928.
HORT, D.
717 *Tahiti: the garden of the Pacific.* London. 1891.
HUÉ, F. and HAURIGOT, G.
718 *Nos petites colonies . . . Taiti et ses dépendances . . .* Paris. 1887.
HUGUENIN, P.
719* *Raiatea la sacrée.* Neuchâtel. 1902.
JACQUIER, H.
720* Le Mirage et l'exotisme tahitiens dans la littérature, *S.E.O.B.*, 7,1, 1-27. 1944.
721** Contribution à l'étude de l'alimentation et de l'hygiene alimentaire en Océanie Française, *S.E.O.B.*, 86, 584-605. 1949.
KEABLE, R.
722 Tahiti tamed and shamed . . ., *Asia*, October. 1924.
723 *Numerous treasure.* New York. 1925.
KEELER, C.
724 Upon a coral strand (Tahiti), *Out West Magazine*, 491-99, 634-44. 1903.
LEBEAU, H.
725 *Otahiti. Au pays de l'éternel été.* Paris. 1911.
LE CHARTIER, H.
726 *Tahiti et les colonies françaises de la Polynésie.* Paris. 1887.
LESCURE, R.
727* Contribution à l'histoire de l'insurrection des Iles-sous-le-Vent, 1846-1897, *S.E.O.B.*, 65, 141-51; 66, 180-95. 1939.
LEVERS, A.
728* Esquisse chronologique de l'histoire de Tahiti et des Iles de la Société, *S.E.O.B.*, 4, 197-213. 1918.
LOTI, P.
729 *Tahiti.* New York (translated by N. H. Hardy). 1927.

MacQuarrie, H.
730   *Tahiti days.* New York. 1920.

Malardé, Y.
731*   Une journée dans la vallée de Tautira, *S.E.O.B.*, 5, 450-58. 1935.
732*   Maeva, îles de Huahine, *S.E.O.B.*, 7, 5, 247-50. 1946.

Marcantoni, P.
733*   Histoire de Huahine . . ., *S.E.O.B.*, 25,26. 1928.

Mayer, A. G.
734*   A history of Tahiti, *Popular Science Monthly*, 1-47. 1915.

Menard, W.
735*   A south sea fish drive, *Natural History*, 56, 400-03. 1948.

Morrison, J.
736*   An account of the island of Tahiti and the customs of the islanders, *Ibid*, 14, 3, 756-60. 1939.

Mühlmann, W. E.
737**   *Die geheime Gesellschaft der Arioi.* Internationales Archiv für Ethnographie, Supplement zu Bd. 32. 1932.

Nordhoff, C.
738**   Notes on the off-shore fishing of the Society Islands, *P.S.J.*, 39, 137-73, 221-62. 1930.

Nordmann, P. I.
739   *Tahiti. Illustrations en couleurs* . . . Paris. 1939.

Orsmond, J. M.
740   Journal, letter-books, and other papers (manuscripts). Mitchell Library, Sydney. 1844-48.

Pétard, P.
741*   La végétation madréporique de district de Teavaro (île Moorea); description et usages de quelques plantes indigènes de Tahiti, *Annuaire de Médecine et de Pharmacie Coloniales*, 37, 76-96. 1939.

Ramsden, E.
742*   Tahiti: a short sketch of the island's discovery, occupation and history, *A.G.* 3, 22-28. 1940.
743*   William Stewart and the introduction of Chinese labour in Tahiti, 1864-1874, *P.S.J.*, 55, 187-214. 1946.

Reeves, E.
744   *Brown men and women* . . . London. 1898.

Rey, L.
745*   Essai de réconstitution des moeurs et coutumes de l'ancien Tahiti . . ., *S.O.J.*, 76, 191-95, 77, 259-63. 1946.

Roberts, H. H.
746*   Modern Tahitian popular songs or Ute, *Publications in Anthropology, Institute of Human Relations, Yale University*. New Haven. 1932.

SELECT BIBLIOGRAPHY 109

ROPITEAU, A.
747* Exposé succinct de l'état actuel de la vie Tahitienne aux îles Tahiti, S.E.O.B., 36, 31-33. 1938.
748** La pêche aux thon (tuna) à Maupiti, S.O.J., 3, 12-21. 1947.
ROTH, H. L.
749* Tatu in the Society Islands, R.A.I.J., 35, 283-94. 1905.
SALMON, E.
750* Les maximes de Tetunae, Revue de Folklore Français et de Folklore Colonial, 1. 1937.
SALMON, T.
751* The history of the island of Borabora and genealogy of our family tree . . . Papeete. 1904.
SCHENCK, E.
752 Come unto these yellow sands. New York. 1940.
SEGALEN, V.
753 Les immémoriaux (novel of early Tahiti). Paris. 1907.
SEURAT, L. G.
754* Sur quelques similitudes des . . . coutumes des indigènes de Funafuti et des indigènes des îles de la Société, et l'archipel de Tuamotus, Linnean Society of New South Wales, Proceedings, 28, 926-31. 1903.
755* Flore économique de la Polynésie française, Société Nationale d'Acclimatisation de France, Bulletin, 310-26, 355-59, 369-76. 1905.
756* Les îles coralliennes de la Polynésie. Société de Géographie de Paris, Bulletin 16, 18-40. 1906a.
757* Tahiti et les établissements français de l'Océanie. Exposition coloniale de Marseille. Paris. (Bibliography of earlier works). 1906b.
SHAPIRO, H. L.
758* Physical characters of the Society Islanders, B.P.M.M., 11, 4. 1930.
STUART, W. J.
759* Atimaono, S.E.O.B., 60, 726-73; 61, 768-78 (1937); 63, 49-65 (1938); 80, 361-66 (1947).
TREAT, I.
760 Tinito in the south seas, Asia, 37, 421-23. 1937.
761* South-sea adventure in the kitchen, The Geographical Magazine, February, 245-58. 1938.
T'SERSTEVENS, A.
761a* Tahiti et sa couronne. 2 vols. Paris. (Includes some materials on Tuamotus, Australs, and Marquesas.) 1950.
VERNIER, C.
762** Pêches et engins de pêche à Tahiti et aux îles Sous-le-Vent, S.O.J., 3,3, 5-11. 1947.
WILDER, G. P.
763* The breadfruit of Tahiti. B.M.B. 50. 1928.

Tuamotus

ALLAN, P.
764   Tuamotu and the Gambier Islands, *Mid-Pacific*, 14, 481-84. 1918.

AUDRAN, H.
765*   Some Paumotu chants, *P.S.J.*, 12, 221-42. (Other folklore materials,
       P.S.J., 1910, 19, 176-94; 1911, 20, 179-84.) 1903.
766*   Moeava, le grand "kaito Paumotu", *S.E.O.B.*, 2, 53-62. 1917.
767*   Napuka et ses habitants, *S.E.O.B.*, 3, 126-36. 1918.
768** Traditions and notes on the Paumotu (or Tuamotu) Islands, *P.S.J.*,
       27, 26-35, 90-92, 132-36; 28, 31-38. 1918-19.
769*   Un glorieux épisode de la vie de Moeava, *S.E.O.B.*, 5, 46-53. 1919.
770*   Noms d'illustres marins Paumotu des temps passés, *S.E.O.B.*, 7, 19-20.
       1923.

BARUCH, M.
771   Tuamotu Archipelago, amongst the pearl divers, *Walkabout*, 23, 45-47.
       1936.

BELTRAN Y ROZPIDE, R.
772   Las islas Tuamotu, *Sociedad Geografica de Madrid, Boletin*, 15, 23-45.
       1883.

BURROWS, E. G.
773** *Native music of the Tuamotus.* B.M.B. 109. 1933.

CAILLOT, A-C. E.
774*   *Histoire des religions de l'Archipel Paumotu.* Paris. 1932.

CHRISTIAN, F. W.
775*   *Eastern Pacific lands.* London. 1910.

COMMISSARIAT GÉNÉRAL DES ETABLISSEMENTS FRANÇAIS DE L'OCÉANIE.
776   *Dans les eaux du Pacifique.* Exposition Coloniale Internationale. Paris.
       1931.

COTTEZ, J.
777*   Note sur Bellinghausen, *S.E.O.B.*, 5, 7, 209-16. 1933.

CURTON, E. DE
778   *Tahiti and French Polynesia.* London. 1943.

CUZENT, G.
779*   Archipel des Pomotu, *Société Académique de Brest, Bulletin*. 2nd series,
       9, 49-90. 1883-84.

EMORY, K. P.
780*   *Tuamotuan stone structures.* B.M.B.118. 1934.
781*   Tuamotuan concepts of creation, *P.S.J.*, 49, 69-136. 1940.
782** *Tuamotuan religious structures and ceremonies.* B.M.B. 191. 1947.
783   Tuamotuan material culture (in preparation).

FRIEDERICI, G.
784   Ein Beitrag zur Kenntnis der Tuamotu-inseln, *Mitteilungen des Vereins
       für Erdkunde zu Leipzig.* 97-176. 1910.

GESSLER, C.
785* Aita fanau, *Asia*, 35, 551-55. 1935a.
786* Napuka, isle of peace, *Asia*, 35, 236-43. 1935b.
787* The dangerous isles, *Pacific Geographic Magazine*, 1, 3, 12-18, 26-28. 1936a.
788* I walked too near a grave, *Asia*, 36, 1, 22-27. 1936b.
789* *Road my body goes*. New York. 1937.
790* *The reasonable life*. New York. 1950.

GUILLOT, F.
791 *Souvenirs d'un colonial en Océanie. Taiti, îles Marquises, Tubuai et Tuamotu* 1888-1911). Annecy. 1935.

HALL, J. N. and NORDHOFF, C. B.
792 *Faery lands of the south seas*. New York. 1921.

HALL, J. N.
793 *Under the south*. London. 1928.

HERVÉ, F.
794 My south sea coral islands, *Asia*, 32, 508-13. 1932.

MAZÉ, P.
795* Histoire d'hier (Tureia and Paraoa islands), *S.E.O.B.*, 31, 279-88. 1929.

MONTITON, A.
796 Les Paumotus, *Les Missions Catholiques*, 6, 339, 341-44, 354-56, 366-67, 378-79, 490-91, 498-99, 502-04. Lyon. 1874.

SCHENCK, E.
797 *Come unto these yellow sands*. New York. 1940.

SEURAT, L. G.
798* Sur quelques similitudes des . . . coutumes des indigènes de Funafuti et des indigènes des îles de la Société, et l'archipel des Tuamotus . . ., *Linnean Society of New South Wales*, 28, 926-31. 1903.
799** Procédés de pêche des anciens Paumotu, *l'Anth.* 16, 295-307. 1905a.
800* L'archipel des Tuamotu et ses habitants. Moeurs des anciens Paumotu, *Revue Coloniale* (n.s.), 28 July, 385-99. 1905b.
801* Les *marae* des îles orientales de l'archipel des Tuamotu, *l'Anth.* 16, 475-84. 1905c.
802* Légendes des Paumotu, *Revue des Traditions Populaires*, 20, 11-12; 21, 2. 1905d.

SHURCLIFF, S. N.
803 *Jungle islands* . . . (record of the Crane Pacific expedition). New York. 1930.

STEVENSON, R. L.
804 *In the south seas* (pp. 140-203). 1890.

STIMSON, J. F.
805** *Tuamotuan religion*. B.M.B. 103. 1933a.
806* *The cult of Kiho-tumu*. B.M.B. 111. 1933b.
807* *Legends of Maui and Tahaki*. B.M.B. 127. 1934.
808* *Tuamotuan legends, the demigods*. B.M.B. 148. 1937.

I

TREGEAR, E.
809   The Paumotuan islands, *P.S.J.*, 2, 195. 1893.

Gambiers (*Mangareva*)

ALAZARD, I.
810   Les îles Gambier, *Annales des Sacrés-Cœurs*. Braine-le-Comte. 1894-98.

BUCK, P. H. (TE RANGI HIROA)
811** *Ethnology of Mangareva*. B.M.B. 157. 1938.

CAILLOT, A-C. E.
812   *Histoire de la Polynésie orientale*. Paris. 1910.

CARET, R.
813   Archipel de Mangaréva, *Revue d'Orient*, 3, 21-33.

CASEY, R. J.
814   Mangareva, in *Easter Island*, 51-68. New York. 1932.

COUTEAUD, P.
815*   Anthropologie et alimentation, *La Presse Médicale*, 80. 1911.

CUZENT, G.
816   *Voyage aux îles Gambier*. Paris. 1872.

DESMEDT, M.
817*   Les funérailles et l'exposition des morts à Mangaréva (Gambier),
        Société des Américanistes de Belgique, Bulletin, 128-36. 1932.

ESKRIDGE, R. L.
818*   *Manga Reva*. Indianapolis. 1931.

GERBAULT, A.
819*   Les peuplements de Mangaréva . . ., *S.E.O.B.*, 13, 59-65. 1926.
820   *L'évangile du soleil*. Paris. (English translation: *Gospel of the sun*. London,
        1933.) 1932.

LAVAL, H.
821*   Les funérailles à Mangaréva (Gambier) . . ., *Société des Américanistes
        de Belgique, Bulletin*, Décembre, 137-147. 1932.
822** *Mangaréva, l'histoire ancienne d'un peuple Polynésien*. Braine-le-Comte.
        1938.

MAIGRET, L. D.
823   History of the kings of Mangareva. *The Polynesian*, 1 December 12,
        19. Honolulu. 1840.

MÉTRAUX, A.
824*   Une féodalité cannibale en Polynésie française (Les îles Gambier et
        l'oeuvre du P.Laval), *Revue de Paris*, October, 637-61. 1937.

MORDVINOFF, N.
825*   Ru a kipo: pei Mangarévien (dancing), *S.E.O.B.*, 6, 4, 131-40. 1945.

MOULY, R. P.
826   *Cannibales à genoux; l'extraordinaire conversion des îles Gambier*. Paris.
        1938.

SMITH, S. P.
827* Notes on the Mangareva or Gambier group of islands, eastern Polynesia, *P.S.J.*, 27, 115-31. 1918.

Australs and Rapa

AITKEN, R. T.
828** *Ethnology of Tubuai.* B.M.B. 70. 1930.
BELTRAN Y ROZPIDE, R.
829 Las islas Cook y Tubuai . . ., *Sociedad Geografica de Madrid*, 15, 326-37. 1883.
BROWN, J. M.
830 Raivavae and its statues, *P.S.J.*, 38, 105-21. 1929.
CAILLOT, A-C. E.
831 *Histoire de l'île Oparo ou Rapa.* Paris. 1932.
DOUGLAS, A. J. A. and JOHNSON, P. H.
832 *The south seas today.* London (Rurutu, Rapa). 1926.
EMORY, K. P.
833* The curved club from a Rurutu cave, *S.E.O.B.*, 5, 12-14. 1932.
GUILLOT, F.
834 *Souvenirs d'un colonial en Océanie . . . Tubuai . . .*(1888-1911). Annecy. 1935.
HILL, H. U.
835* Wood carvings of the Austral Islands, *Journal, University of Pennsylvania Museum*, 12, 179-99. 1921.
SHEPPARD, T.
836* A carved drum from Raivavae (High Island), *Man*, 93, 108-09. 1939.
SMITH, S. P.
837* Easter Island (Rapa-nui) and Rapa (Rapa-iti) Island, *P.S.J.*, 19, 171-75. 1910.
STOKES, J. F. G.
838* Manuscripts on Austral Islands (Bishop Museum).
SUTHERLAND, I. L. G.
839* The hermits of the Austral Islands, *New Zealand Magazine*, Jan.-Feb., 7-8. 1934.
URBAIN, M.
840* Notes sur les pagaies sculptées des îles Tubuai, *S.O.J.*, 3,3, 113-18. 1947.

Marquesas

AHNNE, M. E.
841* De l'usage des échasses aux Marquises, *S.E.O.B.*, 5,14, 508-17. 1935.
ALLMON, C.
842 Shores and sails in the south seas, *National Geographic Magazine*, 97, 73-104. 1950.

ARMSTRONG, R.
843 Sketch of Marquesan character, *Hawaiian Spectator*, 1, 1, 6-16. 1838.

BELTRAN Y ROZPIDE, R.
844 Las islas Marquesas, *Sociedad Geografica de Madrid, Boletin*, 13, 145-70. 1880.

BERCHON, —
845 La tatouage aux îles Marquises, *Société d'Anthropologie de Paris, Bulletin* 1, 99-117. 1884.

BOULE, L. J.
846 Réconstitution du harpon ancien des îles Marquises . . ., *S.O.J.*, 4, 148-51. 1948.

BRIGHAM, W. T.
847* Marquesan and Tahitian homes, *Mid-Pacific Magazine*, October, 393-96. 1916.

CHAULET, R. P. G.
848 Notices géographiques, ethnologiques et réligieuses sur les îles Marquises (5 manuscript packages). Archives de la Maison Mère, Congrégation des Sacrés-Cœurs. Braine-le-Comte.

CHRISTIAN, F. W.
849* Marquesan cosmogony, *P.S.J.*, 4, 187-202. 1895a.
850* Notes on the Marquesans, *P.S.J.*, 4, 187-202. 1895b.
851* *Eastern Pacific lands: Tahiti and the Marquesas*. London. 1910.

CHURCH, J. W.
852* A vanishing people of the south seas, *National Geographic Magazine*, 275-306. 1919.

CLAVEL, A.
853* Dépopulation aux îles Marquises, *Société d'Anthropologie de Paris, Bulletin*, 3rd series, 7, 490-500. 1884.
854* La tatouage aux îles Marquises, *Revue d'Ethnographie*, 3, 138. 1885.
855* *Les Marquisiens*. Paris. 1885.

CLAYSSEN, —
856* Iles Marquises, les maraes, *S.E.O.B.*, 6, 6-10. 1922.

COMMISSARIAT GÉNÉRAL DES ETABLISSEMENTS FRANÇAIS DE L'OCÉANIE.
857 *Dans les eaux du Pacifique*, 201-10. Exposition Coloniale Internationale. Paris. 1931.

CUZENT, G.
858* *Archipel des îles Marquises*. Paris. 1883.

DELMAS, P. S.
859 *Essai d'histoire de la mission des îles Marquises*. Braine-le-Comte. 1911.
860* *La réligion ou le paganisme des Marquisiens*. Braine-le-Comte. 1927.

DES VERGNES EYRIAUD, P. E.
861 *L'archipel des îles Marquises*. Paris. 1877.

DODGE, E. S.
862** *The Marquesas islands collection in the Peabody Museum of Salem: Catalogue with bibliography.* Salem. 1939.

ELBERT, H.
863** Chants and love songs of the Marquesas Islands, *P.S.J.*, 50, 53-91. 1941.

FREEMAN, L. R.
864* The passion play of Hiva-oa, *Sunset*, April, 725-31. 1915.

FROMENT-GUIEYSSE, G.
865* *Iles Marquises.* Rouen. 1914.

GERARD, R. H. D.
866* *La civilisation des îles Marquises.* Paris. 1940.

GIGLIOLI, E. H.
867* *Note etnologiche dalle isole Marchesi.* Rome. 1889.

GUILLOT, F.
868 *Souvenirs d'un colonial en Océanie . . . îles Marquises . . .* (1888-1911). Annecy. 1935.

GUIZOT, M.
869 Les îles Marquises et Taiti, *Mémoires pour servir à l'histoire de mon temps*, 7, 40-117. Paris. 1871 (?)

HAMY, E. T.
870 De l'usage des échasses aux Marquises, *Société d'Anthropologie de Paris, Bulletin*, 3rd Series, 1, 473-77. 1875.

HANDY, E. S. C.
871** *The native culture in the Marquesas.* B.M.B. 9. 1923.
872** *Marquesan legends.* B.M.B. 69. 1930.

HANDY, E. S. C. AND WINNE, J. L.
873** *Music of the Marquesas Islands.* B.M.B.17. 1925.

HANDY, W. C.
874* *Tattooing in the Marquesas.* B.M.B. 1. 1922.
875* *String figures from the Marquesas and Society Islands.* B.M.B. 18. 1925.
876** Kaoha, Marquesan sketches, *The Yale Review*, January. 1925.
877** *L'art des îles Marquises.* Paris. 1938.

HENRY, C.
878* Les îles Marquises, *Société National d'Acclimatisation de France, Revue*, 5, Part 1, 365-77. 1924.

HEYERDAHL, T.
879 Turning back time in the south seas, *National Geographic Magazine*, 79, 109-36. 1941.

LALLOUR, V.
880 Guerre des Marquesas; and other manuscripts. Turnbull Library, Wellington.

LEBRONNEC
881* Itinéraire des îles Marquises, *S.E.O.B.*, 7, 52-57. 1923.

LINTON, R.
882** *The material culture of the Marquesas.* B.M.M. 8, No. 5, 261-467. 1923.
883** Marquesan society, in *The individual and his society* (by Kardiner, A. and associates). New York (with additional analysis by Kardiner). 1939.

MARIN, A.
884   *Au loin: souvenirs de l'Amérique de Sud et des îles Marquises.* Paris. 1891.

MELVILLE, H.
885   *Typee.* London. 1846.
886   *Omoo; a narrative of adventure in the south seas.* New York. 1863.

MENARD, W.
887*   A forgotten south sea paradise, *Asia,* 33, 457-63, 478-80. 1933.

MOULY, R. P.
888*   *Secrets, candeurs et férocités des cannibales.* Paris. 1949.

RADIGUET, M.
889*   *Les derniers sauvages: la vie et les moeurs aux îles Marquises.* Paris. 1882.

ROCHE, J. DE LA
890   Au sujet des idéogrammes marquisiens, *S.E.O.B.,* 76, 7, 264-65. 1946.

ROLLIN, L.
891*   Une race Océanienne: les indigènes des îles Marquises, *Chroniques,* Dec. 29. 1928.
892** *Les îles Marquises.* Paris. 1929.

STEINEN, K. VON DEN
893*   *Reise nach den Marquesas Inseln.* Gesellschaft für Erdkunde, Verhandl., 25. Berlin. 1898.
894*   Marquesanische Knotenschnüre, *Deutsch Gesellschaft Anthropolog. Ethnolog.,* 34, 108-14. Munich. 1904.
895** *Die Marquesaner und ihre Kunst, primitive Südseeornamentik.* Vols. 1 (1925), 2 (1928). Berlin.

STEVENSON, R. L.
896   *In the south seas* (pp. 1-139). 1890.

TAUTAIN, L. F.
897*   Etude sur le mariage, *Société d'Anthropologie de Paris, Bulletin,* 4, 640-51. 1895a.
898*   Etude sur l'anthropologie et les sacrifices humains, *Société d'Anthropologie de Paris, Bulletin,* 7, 443-52. 1895b.
899*   Notes sur l'ethnographie des îles Marquises, *L'Anth.* 7, 543-52. 1896.
900*   Notes sur les constructions et les monuments, *Société d'Anthropologie de Paris, Bulletin,* 8, 538-58, 667-78. 1897.
901** Etude sur la dépopulation de l'Archipel des Marquises, *L'Anth.* 9, 298-318, 418-36. 1898.

VINCENDON-DUMOULIN, A. C. AND DESGRAZ, C.
902   *Iles Marquises ou Nouka-Hiva.* Paris. 1848.

Polynesian Outliers

BEASLEY, H. G.
903** Notes on the fishing appliances from Ongtong Java, *Man*, 37, 58-60. 1937.

FIRTH, R.
904** A dart match in Tikopia, *Oc.*, 1, 64-96. 1930.
905** A native voyage to Rennell, *Oc.*, 2, 179-98. 1931.
906** The meaning of dreams in Tikopia, in *Essays presented to C. G. Seligman*. London. 1934.
907** *We, the Tikopia*. London. 1936a.
907a** Bond-friendship in Tikopia, in *Custom is king. Essays presented to R. R. Marett*, 259-72. London. 1936b.
908** *Primitive Polynesian economy*. London. 1939.
909** *The work of the gods in Tikopia*. London School of Economics and Political Science, Monographs on Social Anthropology, Nos. 1, 2. 1940.
910* Economics and ritual in sago extraction in Tikopia, *Mankind*, 4, 4, 131-42. 1950.

HOGBIN, H. I.
911** The problem of depopulation . . . as applied to Ongtong Java (Solomon Islands), *P.S.J.*, 39, 43-66. 1930a.
912** Transition rites at Ongtong Java, *P.S.J.*, 39, 94-112, 201-20. 1930b.
913** Spirits and healing of the sick in Ongtong Java, *Oc.*, 1, 146-66. 1930-31a.
914** The social organization of Ongtong Java. *Oc.*, 1, 399-425. 1930-31b.
915** Tribal ceremonies at Ongtong Java (Solomon Islands), *R.A.I.J.*, 61, 27-55. 1931a.
916** The sexual life of the natives of Ongtong Java, *P.S.J.*, 40, 23-34. 1931b.
917** Education in Ongtong Java, *A.A.*, 33, 601-14. 1931c.
918* A note on Rennell Island, *Oc.*, 2, 174-78. 1931-32.
919** Sorcery at Ongtong Java, *A.A.*, 34, 441-48. 1932.
920** *Law and order in Polynesia*. London. 1934a.
921* "Polynesian" colonies in Melanesia, *P.S.J.*, 49, 199-220. 1934b.

LAMBERT, S. M.
922* Health survey of Rennell and Bellona Islands, *Oc.*, 2, 136-73. 1931.

LAZARUS, D. M.
923** Live bait fishing in Ongtong Java (with additional notes by H. G. Beasley), *Man*, 37, 57-58. 1937.

MACGREGOR, G.
924** The gods of Rennell Island, in *Studies in the Anthropology of Oceania and Asia . . . in memory of Roland B. Dixon*. Peabody Museum of American Archaeology and Ethnology, Papers, 20, 32-37. 1943.

THILENIUS, G.
925** *Ethnographische Ergebnisse aus Melanesien*, part 1, Die Polynesischen Inseln an der Ostgrenze Melanesiens. Halle. 1902.

VAN DEN BROEK D'OBRENAN, R.
926* Notes sur l'île Rennel et ses Tatouages, *S.O.J.*, 3, 3, 23-33. 1947.

WOODFORD, C. M.
927* Some account of Sikiana . . . , *Man*, 103, 164-69. 1906a.
928* Notes on Leueneuwa, or Lord Howe's group, *Man*, 89, 133-35. 1906b.
929* Notes on Rennell Island, *Man*, 24, 33-37. 1907.
930* On some little-known Polynesian settlements in the neighbourhood of the Solomon Islands, *G.J.*, 48, 26-54. 1916.

Some Collateral Studies

BASCOM, W. R.
931** Ponapean prestige economy, *Southwestern Journal of Anthropology*, 4, 211-21. 1948.

BARNETT, H. G.
932** *Palauan society*. University of Oregon Publications, Eugene (mimeographed). 1949.

BEAGLEHOLE, E.
933** *Some modern Hawaiians*. University of Hawaii Research Publications, 19. 1939.

BEAGLEHOLE, E. AND P.
934** *Some modern Maoris*. New Zealand Council of Educational Research. 1946.

BUCK, P. H. (TE RANGI HIROA)
935** *Material culture of Kapingamarangi*. B.M.B. 200. 1950.

FIRTH, R.
936** *Primitive economics of the New Zealand Maori*. London. 1929.

HANDY, E. S. C.
937** *The Hawaiian Planter*. Vol. I. B.M.B. 161. 1940.

HANDY, E. S. C., PUKUI, M. K., AND LIVERMORE, K.
938** *Outline of Hawaiian physical therapeutics*. B.M.B. 126. 1934.

HAWTHORN, H. B.
939** *The Maori: a study in acculturation*. American Anthropological Association Memoir, 64. 1944.

KEESING, F. M.
940** *Hawaiian homesteading on Molakai*. University of Hawaii Research Publications, 16. 1936.
941** (Editor) *Handbook of the U.S. Trust Territory of the Pacific islands*. Navy Department, Washington (with bibliography). 1949.

LESSA, W. A.
942** *The ethnography of Ulithi atoll*. Pacific Science Board, National Research Council (mimeographed, to be published). 1950.

MASON, L.
943** The Bikinians: A transplanted population, *Human Organization*, 9, 1, 5-15. 1950.

MURDOCK, G. P.
944** *Social organization and government in Micronesia.* Pacific Science Board, National Research Council (mimeographed.) 1949.

MURPHY, R. E.
945** The economic geography of a Micronesian atoll (Mokil), *Association of American Geographers, Annals,* 40, 1, 58–83. 1950.

OLIVER, D. L. (EDITOR)
946** *Planning Micronesia's future; a summary of the United States Commercial Company's Economic Survey of Micronesia,* 1946. Cambridge. 1951.

SPOEHR, A.
947** *Majuro, a village in the Marshall islands.* Chicago Natural History Museum, Fieldiana: Anthropology 39. 1949.

SUTHERLAND, I. L. G. (EDITOR)
948** *The Maori people today.* Wellington (especially important material on land tenure experiments and agriculture). 1940.

THOMPSON, L.
949** *Guam and its people.* Princeton (revised edition). 1947.

USEEM, J.
950** The changing structure of a Micronesian society, *A.A.,* 47, 4. 1945.

INDEX

Community centres, 45, 61
Community development, 41, 44, 63
Community studies, 41, 44, 66
Cook Islands, 9-10; population, 12; agriculture, 15, 32; fisheries, 17-18; hand-crafts, 20; nutrition, 23; transport, 28; land tenure, 29; labour, 31; education, 38; patterns of settlement, 41; housing, 42; social system, 44; accultural processes, 46; ideology and religion, 46-7; folklore, 48; art, 49; emigration, 55; diseases, 57. *See also* Pukapuka
Co-operative activities, 25, 42, 50-1, 63, 66
Co-ordinated Investigation of Micronesian Anthropology, 12
Coulter, J. W., 17, 19
Crampton, H. E., 49
Credit, 26-7, 61-2
Culture contact, 10-11, 13, 21
Currency, 25-7

Damm, H., 49
Death, 58, 66
Demographic research, 12-14, 64
Densmore, F., 49
Diseases, 56-7, 63, 66
Disaster conditions, 54-5
du Bois, Cora, 47

Economic development, emphasis by anthropologists, 8, 16, 21, 64; in Nauru, Ocean and Makatea Islands, 10; hand-crafts, 20-2; trade and commerce, 25-6; Fijian Development Fund, 35
Education, 36-40, 62, 66; of non-indigenous groups, 40
Elbert, H., 49
Elkin, A. P., 1
Ellice Islands, 9-10; population, 12; agriculture, 15; fisheries, 17; hand-crafts, 20; nutrition, 23; transport, 28; land tenure, 29; labour, 30; education, 38; patterns of settlement, 40; housing, 42; social system, 44; ideology and religion, 46; folklore, 48; art, 49; co-operatives, 50; diseases, 57
Ethnology, definition of, 2; descriptive, 3-5
Exchange, 25-6, 64

Fiji, 9-11; population, 12; agriculture, 15-17; fisheries, 17; livestock, 19-20; hand-crafts, 20; nutrition, 22-3; transport, 28; land tenure, 29; labour, 30; smallholding, 34-5, 65; education, 37-8; patterns of settlement, 40-1; housing, 42; social system, 44; ideology and religion, 46, 48; folklore, 48; art, 49; diseases, 56
Firth, Raymond, 8, 12, 23, 25, 30, 37, 41, 44 *n*., 49
Fisheries, 17-19, 61-3
Folklore, 48
Food, habits, 22-5, 61-2, 64; preservation and storage, 24, 61-2
Forestry, 22, 63-4

Gambier Islands, 9; population, 12; agriculture, 15; fisheries, 17; hand-crafts, 20; nutrition, 23; transport, 28; land tenure, 29; labour, 31; patterns of settlement, 41; housing, 42; social system, 44; ideology and religion, 46; folklore, 48; art, 49; diseases, 57

Games, 49-50, 67
Geddes, W. R., 16, 19, 30, 37, 41, 44, 50
Gilbert Islands, 9-10; population, 12; migration, 14; agriculture, 15; fisheries, 17-18; hand-crafts, 20; nutrition, 23; transport, 28; land tenure, 29; housing, 42; social system, 44; ideology and religion, 46; folklore, 48; art, 49; co-operatives, 50; displaced population, 54; diseases, 57
See also Onotoa